The THEFT of WORSHIP

How to Ratify Your Position in Christ
and Frame Your Reality in Truth
By the Language and Lyrics of Your Worship

PAUL ALLEN
with Wendy K. Walters

The THEFT *of* WORSHIP
© 2023 Paul Allen.

All rights reserved. No part of this publication may be reproduced, distributed, or transmitted in any form or by any means, including photocopying, recording, or other electronic or mechanical methods, without the prior written permission of the publisher, except in the case of brief quotations embodied in critical reviews and certain other noncommercial uses permitted by copyright law. For permission requests, please contact the author.

Published by Paul & Yvonne Allen | Southlake, Texas

    ISBN (Paperback): 979-8-9889023-3-1
    ISBN (Kindle): 979-8-9889023-4-8
    Library of Congress Control Number: 2023915818

Printed in the United States of America

Collaborative ghostwriter: Wendy K. Walters | www.wendykwalters.com

Prepared for Publication: www.palmtreeproductions.com

Scripture quotations marked AMP are taken from The Amplified Bible. Copyright © 2015 by The Lockman Foundation, La Habra, CA 90631. All rights reserved.

Scripture quotations marked CSB are taken from the Christian Standard Bible. Copyright © 2017 by Holman Bible Publishers. Used by permission. Christian Standard Bible®, and CSB® are federally registered trademarks of Holman Bible Publishers, all rights reserved.

Scripture quotations marked ESV are taken from The ESV® Bible (The Holy Bible, English Standard Version®), copyright © 2001 by Crossway, a publishing ministry of Good News Publishers. Used by permission. All rights reserved.

Scripture quotations marked KJV are taken from The King James Version of the Bible, which is in the public domain.

Scripture quotations marked MSG are taken from THE MESSAGE, copyright © 1993, 2002, 2018 by Eugene H. Peterson. Used by permission of NavPress. All rights reserved. Represented by Tyndale House Publishers, Inc.

Scripture quotations marked NASB are taken from the New American Standard Bible®, Copyright © 1960, 1971, 1977, 1995, 2020 by The Lockman Foundation. All rights reserved.

Scripture quotations marked NIV are taken from THE HOLY BIBLE, NEW INTERNATIONAL VERSION®, NIV® Copyright © 1973, 1978, 1984, 2011 by Biblica, Inc.® Used by permission. All rights reserved worldwide.

Scripture quotations marked NKJV are taken from the New King James Version®. Copyright © 1982 by Thomas Nelson. Used by permission. All rights reserved.

Scripture quotations marked TPT are from The Passion Translation®. Copyright © 2017, 2018, 2020 by Passion & Fire Ministries, Inc. Used by permission. All rights reserved.

To contact the author:
PAUL@THE29THCHAPTER.COM

ACKNOWLEDGMENTS

PASTOR CAIRO MARQUES—for believing in us from the very beginning.

PASTOR JOSEPH AND DONNA SAPIENZA—for the hours we spent at your kitchen table.

PASTOR ROBERT MORRIS—your seven-part series on words was taken to heart and prepared me to receive the *rhema* that became the inspiration for this book.

JONATHAN SHUTTLESWORTH—for verbalizing what I have known deep in my spirit; putting human words to spiritual realities. Thank you.

DR. KERRY WOOD—your teaching on the Trinity and Their indwelling presence has been so formative in how we have framed our relationship with God.

PASTOR LARRY (DAD) TITUS—for being a father to us.

WENDY K. WALTERS—at your *Release the Writer* seminar, you had me self-prophecy, "My name is Paul Allen, and I am an author."

YVONNE ALLEN—for being there by my side all this time and holding me true to my words.

FATHER, SON, AND HOLY SPIRIT—I love y'all, and I love doing life with You. We are so good together.

The THEFT *of* WORSHIP

> GOD *is* SPIRIT, *and those who* WORSHIP HIM *must* WORSHIP *in* SPIRIT *and* TRUTH.
>
> JOHN 4:24, NKJV

The THEFT *of* WORSHIP

CONTENTS

FOREWORD	1
PREFACE	5
CHAPTER 1 **WHAT WALLS?**	9
CHAPTER 2 **PROGRESSIVE REVELATION**	15
CHAPTER 3 **WORDS CREATE WORLDS**	25
CHAPTER 4 **WHAT IS WORSHIP?**	41
CHAPTER 5 **WHEN YOU PRAY**	53
CHAPTER 6 **THE SUPERNATURAL ON-RAMP**	75
CHAPTER 7 **TO ILLUSTRATE**	89
CHAPTER 8 **COME UP HIGHER**	101
ABOUT THE AUTHOR	111

The THEFT *of* WORSHIP

FOREWORD

I was introduced to Paul Allen while working with his wife, Yvonne, on her first book. We met in a coffee shop in Grapevine, Texas, and from the moment we met, our spirits were in sync. We were not five minutes into our appointment when I knew I would agree to work with him on this project.

There he was, eyes bright, white teeth sparkling in an ever-present smile, joy bubbling from his being as he sipped his tea and talked with great exuberance in his proper British accent about the power of our words and his commitment to using them with great intention.

That's where he had me.

I am careful with my words. Careful with my thoughts. Intentional with them. I literally wrote a book called *Intentionality*! I so value the gift of God in me, the expression of God through me, and the power and purpose of His identity within me that I feel my words must reflect and honor Him—His nature, His character, and His authority. I am His representative on earth. I bear the mark of heaven's brand, and as a Christian—a Christ follower—to speak or act in ways He would not speak or act, but assign His name to it is to take His name in vain.

As Paul and I visited more, discussed theology, and compared notes on several topics, we decided we would be friends. Several months later, my husband and I joined Paul and Yvonne on a trip to the United Kingdom with the purpose of interviewing him for this book, chapter by chapter, so I could capture his heart and wrap language around his charge to you.

I am a ghostwriter and have long viewed ghostwriting as spirit writing because spirit communicates with spirit. If I can connect with a person's spirit, finding their voice is easy. Expressing their heart is natural. It is much the same as when I pray in the Spirit, and my soul wraps language around, finds understanding, and assigns meaning to God's expression to me.

Paul's topic, *The Theft of Worship*, intrigued me. I grew up the daughter of a preacher, and later spent fifteen years as a worship leader for two congregations. We often worshipped spontaneously, and I encouraged people to sing the song of the Lord—wild, free, and authentically expressed from their hearts. My team and I wrote many songs out of whatever series was being preached that reinforced what God was saying to our congregation. They were powerful and relevant to us in that local assembly, and once we had moved to another dimension, we let those songs pass. They were yesterday's manna, and we did not try to store them in jars to grow moldy or have worms. We made no attempt to market them to the masses. They were personal notes between lovers.

FOREWORD

Some songs are ageless. Literally timeless, and whenever they are sung, my heart stirs, my spirit soars, and heaven responds. They build my faith. They strengthen my trust and confirm my theology. I love the energy of corporate worship, and God does too. I enjoy the tribal sense of belonging and the joy of shared community that comes when a group of people lifts their voices together in song. Nothing compares to what happens when unity is in the room—and that is not achieved by a bunch of people standing in a room singing the same words. Unity comes when every spirit in the room is aware, attuned, and connected to God's Spirit, and the sound of heaven fills every heart. Power and purpose intersect, and transformation comes. If you have ever experienced it—even once—you'll know what it is, and you'll never be satisfied with less.

> **Nothing compares to what happens when there is unity in the room—**

Often during congregational singing, I pause as I read the lyrics on the screen and think, "Whoa, I don't think I can sing that!" When I met Paul, I found out I was not alone. Through our interactions, Paul has challenged me to think about my own approach to worship more carefully and view my life in the Spirit even more actively.

Make no mistake; Paul Allen is the author of this book. I served him as a scribe. This is his heart and his testimony, God's revelation to him, and his charge to you. He welcomed and was open to my feedback and was gracious in the places where I gave him pushback. The work is stronger for this. As we progressed,

The THEFT *of* WORSHIP

Paul gave me license to insert a bit of myself in the book—not the usual practice when ghostwriting, but my deep respect for him and his for me opened the opportunity for me to write with him, not just as him. So, rather than an anonymous ghostwriter, I am an invested collaborator.

The manuscript is in Paul's voice, not mine, and I hope you let yourself read it with a crisp, British accent in your mind. Enjoy his wit, his humor, and his no-nonsense candor. As you read, open yourself to challenge some conventions, and if you find yourself wanting to put up walls or resist, pause. Take a deep breath, quiet your mind so your spirit can be dialed in, and read his words through the lens of scripture in the light of truth. Then, weigh it up and see if what Paul invites you to experience with regard to your personal worship expressed to God might not be worth the risk of thinking differently.

WENDY K. WALTERS
Ghostwriter, Author, Editor

PREFACE

WHY THE THEFT OF WORSHIP?

The Theft of Worship seems such a strange title for a book, but it was not my idea; the Holy Spirit gave me the title as He was giving me the mandate to write this book. So ultimately, if you have any questions about the title, take it up with Him—it was His idea.

From my conversations with Him, here's my take: the concept is actually very simple. Words matter. And it doesn't just apply to your speech; it also applies to what you sing.

But why *theft*?

In popular church culture on any Sunday morning, across the nation and across the world, throngs of churchgoers lift praises and worship to God in song. Great. This is good. Traditionally, and in contemporary services, these words are prescribed and popularized by local congregations and recording artists. Many of these songs are very familiar, and as is common in human culture, many people follow the acceptable norm within their community, singing along with the melody. Similarly, in church services or singing in the car with a favorite playlist, well-meaning adherents offer up their worship, but they may not necessarily have engaged with the lyrics being sung to see if they are compatible with biblical theology and God's provision for the born-again believer.

When broaching this subject in a private interview and evaluating lyrics line by line with someone, they often realize that what they have been singing might not match what they actually believe or what is biblically accurate for their position in Christ. In so doing, their offering of *worship* was not actually worship. Either it was not from their own heart, and therefore, it was not their own song, thus disqualifying it as worship, or the words were inaccurate. In this case, the person either did not mean what they were singing or worse, they were singing that which was not true—singing lies. Yikes. This is not good. Lying … to God … in church! If you do not mean what you sing or if you sing untrue things, it is not good—it is definitely not worship.

The enemy has always wanted to take worship for himself.[1] If he tried to do this directly, it would be too obvious, so deception is his weapon of choice to intercept or *steal* the worship being offered. What the worshiper thought was being offered as worship to God was being stolen because the intent of their heart was not adequately verbalized, so the transmission of devotion was being stolen.

Let me illustrate. Back in the days of mailing a gift to someone you loved, words were written on the package. We called it the

PREFACE

address. If the address written on the package—the *words*—is written incorrectly, then the gift that is lovingly placed inside the package will not be received by the intended recipient. The sender of the gift had the right motive and love, as proven by the gift being sent. But if the words written on the package are incorrect, then the intended addressee would not be the recipient of the act of worship, in this case, the gift.

If our enemy can cause the sender (the worshipper) to use an incorrect address (inaccurate words as lyrics on the package), then that gift (worship) will not get to the correct recipient—the Triune God. It would be lost in transit, essentially *stolen* from the One to whom it was intended.

Christian worshipers package things for their Heavenly Father, but if they fail to accurately verbalize, i.e., using the right words in their address, it exposes their worship to theft.

If our enemy can cause the sender (the worshipper) to use an incorrect address (inaccurate words as lyrics on the package), then that gift (worship) will not get to the correct recipient— the Triune God.

Many people genuinely love God. But when it comes to their speech and often in their worship, the words they speak or sing can cause their worship to be stolen. It's very subtle, but it's real: *The Theft of Worship*.

The THEFT *of* WORSHIP

For clarity, this book is focused specifically on *worship*—your words expressed directly to God in adoration. This manuscript does not address praise, declarations, creeds, devotionals, or other biblical recitations. Those are separate and different in application than our expression of worship to the Lord.

BIBLICAL REFERENCES

The book contains copious biblical references pointing you to God's written Word. To keep them from breaking the flow of the narrative, we have chosen to use endnotes to cite them. Great care was taken in every selection, and the references should not be taken as random isolated verses out of context. I encourage you to look at them in their context and cross-referencing. Just as the Bereans were of more noble character, we invite you to do likewise. Please evaluate what is being said against the weight of scripture as you invite the Holy Spirit to lead you into all truth.[2]

Rather than glibly follow popular church culture or run to the safety of that which has been familiar, we invite you to take what is written in this book to the Holy Spirit, ask Him to shed His light on what is being shared, and see if there are any action items or ideological shifts that He may lead you to implement.

ENDNOTES
1. See Isaiah 14:14.
2. See John 16:13.

CHAPTER 1

WHAT WALLS?

I stood one Sunday morning in the auditorium of a large church near our home in Texas. Talented, professional musicians were playing and leading together in song, and the words were up on large screens so congregants could easily follow along. Like everyone else, I was singing too, just as I always did.

But today, something was different.

For weeks, I had been meditating on the power of words. The pastor had delivered a series on this topic, and the message had resonated in my belly. I had long been disciplined in my speech, knowing that the quality of my life depended on the words I released from my mouth. I know that death and life are in the power of the tongue and that from the produce of my lips, I am filled.[1] The quality of my life is linked to the quality of my words. So, these truths were not new concepts in any way, but the connection between my heart and my mouth crystallized.

As I spent time in the Word and sought the Holy Spirit regarding my words, my conviction of their spiritual power grew.

Christ lives in me, and I am in Him.[2] Any word I release that is not in agreement with Him releases death. Only the words I release in agreement with Him—His nature, His character, His goodness, His power—releases life. That every idle word I speak must be accounted for and that, by my words, I am either justified or condemned[3] weighed on me. This biblical truth became a present, intentional reality for me.

Idle words, I pondered. *God, what does that mean?*

My relationship with Jesus had grown so dear that I felt His Spirit say to me, "Paul, you can only speak in agreement with what I say."

I took this literally.

When I was born again, it was a union with Christ. So I began measuring my speech by the reality of this—Christ in me, the hope of glory,[4] with the understanding that all authority had been given to me[5] and that because Jesus lives inside me, I and the Father are one.[6] Like Jesus, I don't speak from my own initiative or authority—I can only say what the Father has told me to say.[7] As I was singing that morning,

WHAT WALLS?

it dawned on me that the words of this song, while they may have been very meaningful to the person who penned them and may have reflected an authentic moment when the author was wrestling in his soul, did not agree with my position or authority in Christ. I stopped singing, carefully considering what I had been mindlessly releasing in song as I followed the lyrics up on the screen.

I could not say those words. They were not congruent with who I was in Christ. I could not *say* those words; therefore, I could not *sing* those words either.

My spirit could not agree with the message. Christ would not be singing this song.

"Why are you still wandering around walls and waiting for them to fall?" God whispered. *"Are they not already down? Who put them back up?"*

"I don't have any walls," I answered Him. "You don't have any walls, so I can't have any walls. I am seated with You in heavenly places,[8] and if I am seated, I can't possibly be walking around walls. To do so would require me to step outside of the finished work of Christ.[9] Why would I do that?"

I looked around and saw hundreds of people singing, many with arms lifted, eyes closed, earnestly "worshipping" as they sang words about barriers and struggle. How could that be worship?

It could not.

From that moment, I altered how I engaged in the corporate expression of praise and worship—the "song portion" of a service or gathering.

It has made all the difference in the world because when I began speaking like Christ, I soon found myself living like Christ and truly embodying what John said, "As He is, so are we in this world."[10] To a large degree, I am living in "heaven on earth," and heaven is manifesting in my personal life, health, marriage, family, and business. I don't think this blessing is for me only, but it is universally accessible to anyone who will embrace not just what Jesus *has said* but what He *is saying* to you right now through the Holy Spirit and in line with His written Word.

Whether or not you recognized the song I spoke of, as you read my experience in that service, and the change that took place when I began speaking like Christ, I believe something inside of you just quickened—even if it was just a pause to consider if what I am saying might be true. Deep in your spirit, you know there is so much more to be enjoyed here and now.

AN INVITATION

With your permission, in these pages, I will challenge some preconceived and popular concepts within modern church culture. I invite you to read with an open heart, and rather than immediately running back to the safety of what everyone in

WHAT WALLS?

mainstream Christianity practices, please weigh this revelation I am about to share against scripture.

Take it to the Holy Spirit to see what He will say to you.

This message is not intended for brand-new or immature believers. A solid biblical foundation is necessary for this publication to have value. This book lovingly questions the modern, western Christian expression of "worship" and invites you into an incredible, life-changing experience that will forever alter your perspective on worship, opening the portal to living an abundant life[11] and walking in kingdom realities. It will help you bring heaven to earth.

Are you willing to be challenged?

Then read on.

The THEFT *of* WORSHIP

ENDNOTES

1. See Proverbs 18:20-21.
2. See Galatians 2:20.
3. See Matthew 12:36-37.
4. See Colossians 1:27.
5. See Matthew 28:18-20.
6. See John 10:29-31.
7. See John 12:49-50 NIV.
8. See Ephesians 2:6.
9. See John 17:4.
10. 1 John 4:17, NIV.
11. See John 10:10.

CHAPTER 2

PROGRESSIVE REVELATION

Wise King Solomon wrote, "It is the glory of God to conceal a matter, but the glory of kings is to search out a matter."[1] Since creation, mankind has been the fortunate recipient of an increasingly informed knowledge of his Creator. There was a precious intimacy between God and man in the Garden of Eden, but to a large degree, this human-divine proximity was severed when sin entered the scene. The ancients had little idea as to who God was. Abraham did not have much to go off when God called him to leave his home country and go to a land that would be shown to him.[2] Job, a contemporary of the patriarchs, yearned for someone to mediate between man and God.[3] When God commissioned Moses to deliver His people, Moses asked, "Whom shall I say has sent me?"[4] Again, there was no precedent.

Throughout Old Testament history God progressively revealed Himself until He finally sent His Son, born of a woman,[5] who was the very express image of God[6] and in whom dwelled the fullness of the Godhead.[7] But after Jesus came, did the progressive revelation stop? Did God change His nature or His way of bringing us to Himself?

No.

Even in the New Testament writings, progressive revelation was still taking place. In the Gospels, Jesus came only for the lost sheep of Israel,[8] and therefore, it was not right to take the children's bread and give it to the Canaanite woman—whom He inferred was a dog. That's not the Gospel that is preached today.

Even after Pentecost, it was a Jewish-only church until the Jerusalem Council, where Gentile converts to Christianity were accepted and not required to keep Mosaic law.[9] This certainly illustrates progressive revelation. So, has the progress stopped? Has God changed His desire to fully reveal himself? Historically, time always reveals more of The Truth (uppercase *The Truth* intended), whether it's through archeology or science.

Because God is a revealer by nature, some things are known today that may not have been readily accessible fifty years ago. Or a hundred. Or even a thousand years ago. We are meant to be always learning, and the process of learning is a revealing of a truth that was there all along. It isn't new; we just know it now. Moreover, when it comes to any form of learning, we must use the premise of what is already known as building blocks to explain what is yet to be learned.

> **When it comes to any form of learning, we must use the premise of what is already known as building blocks to explain what is yet to be learned.**

Think of it like this: in mathematics, you must first learn the concept of numbers and counting. Only after you understand the value assigned to numbers can you learn addition, followed by subtraction. If a teacher began your introduction to mathematics with multiplication or long division before making sure you had the foundation of counting, addition, and subtraction, you would become so confused and frustrated; you would never venture near the subject and miss out on the benefits, blessings, and possibilities that an understanding of mathematics brings to your life.

How about algebra, calculus, geometry, or trigonometry? Would it be possible to learn and practice any of these subjects without a solid foundation of counting, addition, subtraction, multiplication, and division?

Of course not.

Throughout history, each time there is a new "move of God," it is invariably resisted by whatever ecclesiastical or evangelical standard occupies the day. Jesus Himself was resisted by the religious authorities of His day, even though they had studied and had been looking for and awaiting His arrival for centuries.

The "mainstream" usually rejects what is "new" because it confronts what the majority has practiced until it has crystalized into normality and become the accepted tradition. Everything mainstream was once new, perhaps even radical.

When Martin Luther posted his *95 Thesis* on the door of Castle Church in Wittenberg, he challenged the practice of indulgences—that you could pay money for the commutation of the penalty of sin—and pointed out the priesthood of all believers, therefore threatening papal authority. He was seen as a heretic, and wars were fought that turned all of Europe on its head.

The Anglican Church (Church of England) was formed in Luther's wake. It was basically a reformed version of Catholicism. They hold that the way to salvation is in leading a life that reflects the teachings of Jesus, to practice the sacraments of baptism (infant baptism) and the Eucharist (or Holy Communion). They believe their salvation is secured through behavior and practice. So, when George Whitfield, a prominent Anglican, began preaching about the need for a transformative religious conversion he coined the New Birth (salvation by grace through faith); it put him at odds with the faith leaders of the day and led to the First Great Awakening.

PROGRESSIVE REVELATION

George Whitfield, John Wesley, and Jonathan Edwards rocked the world with the teachings of sanctification and perfect love. New hymns were written, reflecting the new revelation and understanding of doctrine. Wesley taught about the "second blessing," which John Fletcher later called the "baptism in the Holy Spirit," though they did not embrace speaking in tongues. These leaders paved the way for the Pentecostal Movement of the Nineteenth Century.

The American Holiness Movement saw an entirely new hymnody produced, focused on celebrating the second blessing and being imbued with power from on High. The new songs released the revealed truth. William Seymore, a black Holiness preacher who became the pastor of the Azusa Street Mission, was an early pioneer of the Pentecostal Movement. He prayed earnestly, believing God was ready to send a new Pentecost, a latter-day outpouring like the book of Acts—Spirit baptism, speaking in tongues, signs, wonders, and miracles.

Like the prophets of old, men and women of God who are hearing His current voice and reaching into the revelation He is awakening within them are usually ridiculed or persecuted. Perhaps they are no longer stoned to physical death, but instead, they are sidelined as being "fringe," "dangerous," or even "heretical" and discredited. Very few people take them seriously.

Time reveals the truth of their revelation, and for many, any celebration of their contribution to the body of Christ progressing comes posthumously. Very few know wide affirmation while pioneering. Their ideas don't often become mainstream until long after they have gone.

I am not saying that what I am about to share is on the level of the kind of shaking and reformation brought to the Church by Martin Luther, George Whitfield, or William Seymore. I am trying to show you from history that God's nature is to reveal, and if your heart is open, you will be able to recognize and receive what God is saying today.

Progressive revelation holds that the things God has revealed to humanity were not given all at once but rather in stages. The Old Testament holds truth; the New Testament does not negate this, but it builds on that foundation and expands our understanding and practice of truth. We could never enter into the New Covenant without the foundation of the Old Covenant. The latter expands the former.

Progressive revelation holds that the things God has revealed to humanity were not given all at once but rather in stages.

The Apostle Mark said it like this, "For the earth bringeth forth fruit of herself; first the blade, then the ear, after that the full corn in the ear."[10]

If we go only by what God has said and not what He is saying, then Abraham would have killed Isaac.

PROGRESSIVE REVELATION

God told Abraham to take his son, Isaac, and sacrifice him on the mountain as a burnt offering. That sounds bizarre to us, but God had a reason for this instruction, and it had nothing to do with Isaac. Had Abraham stood only on what God *had said* and not continued to attune his ear to what God *would say next*, he would not have heard the angel of the Lord say, "Abraham! Abraham! ... Do not lay a hand on the boy ... Do not do anything to him."[11]

Isaac (like Jesus) was a beloved and long-awaited son born under miraculous circumstances. Like Jesus, Isaac's father asked him to carry the wood, the instrument of his death, on his back, and he obediently followed this command. Then God provided a substitute for the sacrifice—a lamb. The whole passage points to Jesus. It is an Old Testament prophetic act of things to come. The progressive revelation of this passage is found in the New Testament with the redemption Jesus would bring. "God Himself will provide the lamb ..."[12]

If Joseph had stopped at what God *had said* and did not lean into what He *was saying*, he would have acted as a good Jew, trained in and abiding by the Law, and divorced Mary. In fact, he was within his legal rights to have her stoned. If he had done so, Jesus would have never been born, or been born as an illegitimate child and never allowed to enter the Temple where He was "about His Father's business."[13]

If Paul had stopped at what God *had said* and was not attuned to what He *was saying*, he would never have taken his missionary journey to Asia. Similarly, Peter was a good Jew who kept the Law and had never eaten anything non-Kosher in his life. That was the instruction God gave them in Leviticus. But in Acts, God said to him, "Rise, Peter; kill and eat."[14]

Peter clung to what God *had said*, seeing it as immovable, and answered, "Not so, Lord! For I have never eaten anything common or unclean."[15]

But God had *new instructions* for Peter, a progressive revelation, if you will. The voice answered Peter's argument by saying, "What God has cleansed, you must not call common."[16]

If Peter had gone by what God *had said* and not what He *was saying*, he would never have tasted bacon.

It was progressive revelation that allowed Gentiles free access to "the way,"[17] even though earlier, Jesus had said He came only for the lost sheep of Israel.[18]

Think about it—God's revelation of Himself to David was greater than it had been to Abraham. David had the benefit of beginning with and building from where Abraham, Isaac, and Jacob left off. Matthew and Mark knew God in a way that Isaiah and Malachi could not imagine.

> **You must start with what you know to be able to learn what you do not yet comprehend.**

You must start with what you know to be able to learn what you do not yet comprehend. Everything we know about God

PROGRESSIVE REVELATION

is only possible because He reveals it to us. It is progressive in nature.

Deep in your belly, you know this is true. You know there is more.

Your heart has heard the cry, and your spirit longs to respond, search out the depths of God's richness, and explore His heart toward you. You were created to live in the finished work of Christ, in the land of "already done," where you are seated with Him in heavenly places, and He has made your enemies a footstool for your feet.[19] This is a place where you can speak to the mountain and see it removed.[20] You are meant always to triumph and have the victory.[21]

You were created to have life and life more abundantly.[22]

If this is not your experience, but your heart yearns for it, then let your spirit declare, "I want in on this."

The THEFT *of* WORSHIP

ENDNOTES

1. Proverbs 25:2, NIV.
2. See Genesis 12:1.
3. See Job 9:33.
4. See Exodus 3:13-15.
5. See Galatians 4:4.
6. See Colossians 1:15.
7. See Colossians 1:19.
8. See Matthew 15:24.
9. See Acts 15:1-31.
10. Mark 4:28, KJV.
11. See Genesis 22:11-12.
12. See Genesis 22:8.
13. See Luke 2:49.
14. Acts 10:13, NKJV.
15. For the full account, see Acts 10:12-15.
16. Acts 10:15, NKJV.
17. See Romans 1:16 and 15:8-13.
18. See Matthew 15:24.
19. See Psalm 110:1 and Acts 2:34-35.
20. See Mark 11:23.
21. See 1 Corinthians 15:57 and 2 Corinthians 2:14.
22. See John 10:10.

CHAPTER 3

WORDS CREATE WORLDS

In the simplest form, a word is a sound or combination of sounds that function as a principal carrier of meaning.[1] String them together, and you have language—communication. Through the filter of literature, words form connections that express creativity, identity, culture, and perspective. If we look at language through a sociological lens, we see that words allow us to communicate thoughts from one person to another. The meaning of these words is encoded by the transmitter (the one speaking) and decoded by the recipient (the one hearing them). Words are the transmission of our thoughts into actions. In fact, language is what makes thought and reason possible. If we study language through the filter of philosophy, we find that words are what form the relationship between meaning and truth—creating understanding.

The THEFT *of* WORSHIP

Words are critical to belief. How else can you express it?

So, the meaning of words is essential to what we believe, what we understand, and how we communicate. As long as you and I both have the same meaning attached to the words we are speaking, we can understand one another without an issue. But the same word can have different meanings for different people. In the U.S., for example, a biscuit is a buttery, flaky, baked bread. But in the U.K., a biscuit is a cookie. A solicitor is a salesman in the States but a lawyer in Britain. In America, mist means fog or drizzle, while in Germany, it means manure—hardly the same thing. Even in the *same* country, you can't expect everyone to use the same words and mean the same things. For example, if I say, "Give me some sugar!" in the Northern United States, I just requested the sweet, granulated stuff, but if I am in the South, I probably just asked someone for a kiss.

A singular word or phrase often has a range of meanings. Different words have different meanings to different people in different cultures, and that's before we even consider slang or discuss industry-specific language—not to mention the vast range of "religious" terms encountered in Christian circles.

Your words are containers of intention and meaning. They hold and carry these concepts just as a bucket carries water. Words are containers of your thoughts—your *psyche*. If you wish to communicate something to someone, you have a

Your words are containers of intention and meaning.

perception in your heart that goes to your mind, where you encode it into words. Your *psyche*, your soul, wraps language around your intent so you can speak your thoughts out loud. Your words hold your thoughts and beliefs, and for you to release words from your mouth, it requires your breath—your *pneuma*—air in motion, wind. Your spirit, *pneuma*, is carried by your words. From this, we draw the conclusion that words are spirit containers.

SPIRIT CONTAINERS

If words are spirit containers, they hold and harness great and endless power because spirit never dies. Consider this:

"In the beginning, God said ..."[2]

God's Spirit was contained in His words, and when He released them, light and life were created. God's words contained His Spirit, and He poured them forth from His lips to perform His will. His words were irrevocable, and they contained creative power. The prophet Isaiah said it like this:

"So shall My Word be that goes forth from My mouth;
It shall not return to Me void, but it shall accomplish
what I please, and it shall prosper in the thing for which
I sent it."[3]

When our words are released, they accomplish what we sent them out to do. Scientifically speaking, our words carry a frequency—vibrations and sound waves. Through "cymatics" (the science of visualizing audio frequencies), scientists can view the patterns of someone's words and know if they are expressing shame, regret, despair, anger, anxiety, hostility, or pain. They can also tell if someone is expressing cheer, gratitude, effervescence, love, peace, or joy. This phenomenon is called the law of frequency and vibration.[4] Our words are actual wavelengths—energy—and they carry creative power. Words are spirit containers of power—for good or for evil, and spirit lasts forever; it never dies. When that spirit comes out of your mouth, it doesn't evaporate. Your words don't just fizzle into nothing, they go out into the spirit world, and they *will* create something. They will prosper in the thing for which you sent them. So, you had better send them out to do something you want done.

> **God is Spirit, and we are made in His image. He is Spirit, and so are we.**

God is Spirit, and we are made in His image. He is Spirit, and so are we. He speaks to us from the abundance of His heart. Words are His gift to us to do the same, and from the abundance of our hearts, our mouths speak.[5]

Some people mindlessly release things like, "I'm so tired," or "I am so overwhelmed," not realizing that by saying these things out loud, they are coming into agreement with it until it becomes their reality. Of course, this isn't intentional. No one really wants to be tired or overwhelmed, anxious, or stressed. But all around us, people are encouraged to express their anxiety and every negative feeling as an avenue to improve their mental health. Now, I'm not against processing the pain of trauma or grieving loss with someone who is loving you through a hard season. Why else would Paul have written to "encourage (comfort) one another and (edify) build one another up?"[6] But a pattern of *expressing* negative things results in a pattern of *experiencing* negative things.

For example, if a child has been told they are slow or stupid, they begin to believe this. When they encounter a new or difficult concept in school, they *speak* words like, "I'm too dumb to understand," or "I'll never be able to get this." The resulting action is that they give up and don't try, thus fulfilling their own prophecy and confirming their belief that they are stupid, slow, or not as smart as others.

If that same child has been told they are intelligent and smart, they will believe it. And when they encounter a new or difficult concept in school, they will *speak* words like, "This is hard, but I'm smart," and "I can do this!" The resulting action is that they will try until they master it, self-fulfilling prophecies here as well. Knowing that they tackled something hard and overcame it will solidify their belief that they are smart and build resilience.

In both scenarios, the power of words made the difference.

As Christians, we are meant to be salt and light in the world.[7] Our saltiness slows down the decay around us and makes people hunger and thirst for what we have. Our light dispels the darkness, and because God is our light source, we spread Christ wherever we go. But many Christians live no differently than unbelievers. Sometimes, they live out an even lower standard of abundant life than the world. Their lamp is dim, and their life is unsavory. It can be tough to convince an unbeliever that you are filled with abundant life—joy, peace, grace, and strength—if your attitudes, disciplines, relationships, and outcomes look no different than theirs. How can your life be abundant if the words proceeding from your mouth are filled with problems, complaints, anxiety, fear, regret, shame, anger, and disappointment?

I call this the John 10:10 conflict. The thief has one aim—to steal, kill, and destroy. Jesus came that we might have life and that life more abundantly.[8] If you are a born-again believer, and Christ—the hope of glory—lives in you, and you are not living an abundant life, then you are in active conflict right now. You are living in between what Jesus said are your rights and entitlements in Christ Jesus—and the reality of your daily life. Your speech is probably the source of this tension. If there is a gap, its source may be caused by the words you speak.

Let's close that gap.

> *"Death and life are in the power of the tongue, and those who love it will eat its fruit."*[9]

This verse is so familiar to many that it has become common, and once something is seen as common, it is easily overlooked or taken for granted. If speaking death over our lives and circumstances is common, would it not be better if our profession of faith grew to be uncommon? What if speaking life—and *only* speaking life—became your regular practice?

WORDS CREATE WORLDS

My wife and I have an uncommon profession of faith, and therefore, we have an uncommon outcome.

I shared in the first chapter how when I got born again, it was a union with Christ. I am in Him, He is in me, and we are one.¹⁰ I desire that when you encounter me, you encounter Jesus. I am seated with Him in heavenly places, in the finished work of Christ.¹¹ I am not just a believer; I am a believing believer. I have no fear because I know who I am.

I am in Him, He is in me, and we are One. I am seated with Him in heavenly places, in the finished work of Christ.

My mind is on the things above, not on circumstances that may surround me. I am seated with Christ at God's right hand. The devil may seek to steal, kill, and destroy me. He can look all he wants, but he cannot find me because I am hidden with Christ in God.¹²

What I release from my mouth—the words I speak—reflect this reality.

In our family and in our business, we have an accurate speech policy. We choose our words carefully and say only what we mean. We always keep our word. Because we always keep our word, we have a good name. Because we keep our word and our commitments, we have a good credit score (the numerical evaluation of how well you keep your word). As a result, we also have "good credit"—credibility, if you will. Our good name attracts money. Banks line up to give us money. Investors are confident in us. Contractors enjoy doing business with us because they know that our word is our bond. Good credit will cause any business to accelerate and prosper. We flourish and live an abundant life because of our diligence regarding the words we speak with our mouths and the actions we take to qualify our speech. The life we now live is a natural manifestation of our spoken spiritual reality.

We understand that our words shape our reality. Words create worlds,[13] and the words we speak sets the framework for the world that we engage with.[14] Not meaning to speak death over something does not alter the consequence of having spoken death. Careless words have real consequences, so being intentional about what we will and will not say is a value we hold dear.

This principle of being intentional with the words you speak holds true for health, wealth, relationships, or any area of your life. So, in our home, we do not rehearse sickness or disease because we don't want to make these things any bigger. The more you talk about something, the more substance you give to it. Out of the heart, the mouth speaks,[15] and so because my heart is born-again—I'm in Christ, and He lives in me—my speech is Christ-like. If you spend time with me for a week or two, all you will ever hear is life, love, laughter, and everything else pertaining to godliness. So why not talk about

> **The more you talk about something, the more substance you give it.**

health and wealth, strength, and vitality? Talk life. As He is, so are we.[16] So speak like Jesus is speaking now, and you will find yourself living in the framework of the world that you have created by your own speech.

People might say something like this to me to push back, "But I'm just discussing real-world problems, not some fairy tale situation. I live in the real world."

So do I. I live on the same planet that you do, but my perceptions may be different, and my experiences may be different because of the fundamental embracing of union with Christ, speaking only as He speaks and, as a result, living as He lives.

This was not always the case in my life, but ever since I embraced what I am sharing in this book, we have found ourselves living in the reality of what we spoke yesterday. Our words have been and continue to be a forth-telling of what is and is to come. They contain creative power, so we are living today, here and now, in the reality of what we have released by the words we have spoken. This can be your experience as well. What is it that you are saying?

WHAT'S ON THE LABEL?

Have you ever met someone diligent with their diet and exercise? Have you ever noticed how careful they are about what they ingest? They are cautious not to eat or drink anything detrimental to their health. They have paid attention to their bodies and know what gives them energy and vitality. They are not slaves to their taste buds but consider how what they consume will affect their health. When they look at the list of ingredients on a health and wellness drink, they carefully evaluate each individual ingredient to ensure that among all the good ingredients, there are no additives mixed in to prolong the shelf life or enhance the appearance. They only want to drink something that is one hundred percent beneficial and has no trace of toxins. These people carefully look at labels and consciously decide whether or not they will buy and consume the product.

It would be nice to see such diligence with things of the Spirit.

Many people have grown accustomed to having high cholesterol, high blood pressure, heart disease, diabetes, joint pain, and poor rest, to name a few. They have also normalized being afraid, anxious, depressed, in debt, stressed, disappointed, having low fulfillment, and spiritual lethargy. In the same way that what we ingest can lead to obesity and hinder our physical health, what we speak from our mouths can lead to spiritual heaviness and impact our spiritual health.

Stay with me in this metaphor for a moment.

What if you read the label on a bottle, and out of ninety-nine ingredients, one of them was arsenic? Or what if one ingredient was human feces? Would you drink it? Would you want to ingest everything on that label? Probably not.

This applies to your spirit, too. What are you listening to? Looking at? What are you reading and bringing into your spirit man? Because what you are taking in will be what you send out. If you send out nine good things, but the tenth is pure poison, you still release death over your life. It only takes a tiny percentage of arsenic for it to be a fatal dose. It's the same thing in the spirit and in your speech. It takes only a tiny percentage of poison, say 1%, to offset the benefit of the 99%. Death and life are in the power of the tongue. Only from pure speech can you have a pure life. You must be born again, and you must only speak from that new nature. The old nature is dead. Don't resurrect it by your speech.

Only from pure speech can you have a pure life.

SPEECH AND OUTCOME

If you are not living an abundant life, and if your outcomes are not what you desire, you can begin right now, today, to adjust your words, and you will see a turnaround.

You can close the gap.

When the Israelites got within striking distance of the Promised Land, Moses sent out twelve men—one from each tribe—to survey the situation and bring back a report so he would know what he was up against before they moved inside the border.

The men spent forty days checking out the situation. They cut down a branch with a cluster of grapes so large it had to be carried on a pole between two of the men. They gathered pomegranates and figs; they witnessed abundant cattle, grain, thriving cities and civilization—a land "flowing with milk and honey,"[17] they reported. But ten of those men focused on the obstacles and their circumstances, forgetting that taking this land was the promise of the One who had brought them out of Egypt, divided the Red Sea before them, and fed them manna in the wilderness. So, they *said* that it was impossible to take the land. "All the people whom we saw in it are men of great stature. There we saw the giants … and we were like *grasshoppers* …"[18]

Only Joshua and Caleb *said*, "… it is an exceedingly good land … God will bring us into this land and give it to us … do not rebel against the Lord, nor fear the people of the land, for they are our bread; their protection has departed from them, and the Lord is with us."[19]

In essence, they *said*, "We can do this, guys. The land is ours—let's go take it!"

The report from the majority was wrong. The majority report of God's chosen people, under God's protection, provision, and care, was wrong.

> **What is right is not always popular, and what is popular is not always right.**

What is right is not always popular, and what is popular is not always right.

Most Christians go along with the popular, majority assessment of the situation. People wring their hands over the culture wars, politics, the economy, wars, pandemics, interest rates ... they agree with the ten and say, "We are like grasshoppers against this world; we don't really stand a chance." And so that becomes their reality.

But there is nothing we cannot do. There is nothing I cannot do because greater is He that is in me than he that is in the world.[20] This is the report I have engraved on my heart, and I make sure that any words I speak are in agreement with what God is saying.

In your network of friends and family, do you have someone who talks negatively all the time? What is the fruit of their life? You can clearly evaluate someone's life by how they speak.

I met with a gentleman that a colleague suggested I work with. He was recommended to me to do business with him, but because of the way he talks, I have no desire to engage in a working relationship with him. His mouth is full of sarcasm. He says things for effect and uses hyperbole to exaggerate. I am old enough and experienced enough to know that there will be subsequent repercussions when someone speaks like this. When people are careless with their words, their lives end up in a mess. I have no desire to link my outcomes to someone who has little or no regard for the power of the words they wield.

Our speech is directly tied to our outcomes.

Our speech is directly tied to our outcomes.

The THEFT *of* WORSHIP

WE GET WHAT WE SAY

The Kingdom of God is voice-activated. Again and again, God said, "Let there be," and there was. Satan knows this, too. When he tempted Jesus in the wilderness, he said, "If you are the Son of God, command these stones to become bread."[21]

Jesus answered him by *saying*, "It is written, 'Man shall not live by bread alone, but by every word that proceeds out of the mouth of God.'"[22]

The enemy who is out to kill your dreams, steal your inheritance, and destroy your destiny understands that the words you say out of your mouth are the key to his diabolical mission. He understands that if you speak death, his job is done. He floods the earth with dead things—ideologies, philosophies, religion, temptations, and songs over the radio, hoping that you will come into agreement with them, take them into your heart until you release them from your mouth, and bring death to your spirit.

The enemy knows that if you speak life and come into agreement with God's character, nature, and provision, it's game over for him. You will be beyond his reach, and he will be unable to touch a single hair on your head.

Words.

Life.

God speaks only life-giving, life-sustaining, life-generating words, and His Kingdom is established by His words.

I have no desire to undo with my mouth what God has done for me by Christ's blood.

I am a child of the covenant.[23]

I am a new creation.[24]

I am a priest and a king.[25]

> **I have no desire to undo with my mouth what God has done for me by Christ's blood.**

I am commissioned to do greater works than Jesus, and whatever I ask in His name that the Father may be glorified, He will do.[26]

God has given me authority over the power of the enemy, over principalities and powers.[27]

God has commanded me to "Be fruitful and multiply; fill the earth and subdue it; have dominion over the fish of the sea, over the birds of the air, and over every living thing that moves on the earth."[28]

We get what we say. By our words, we are justified, and by our words, we will be condemned.[29] So, what we say really matters.

And if what we say is important, then what we sing must be equally important. Let's examine this a little further.

The THEFT *of* WORSHIP

ENDNOTES

1. Word. Retrieved from https://www.dictionary.com/browse/word on June 19, 2023.
2. Read Genesis 1:1-31 for the full creation account. Pay attention to how often you read, "And God said."
3. Isaiah 55:11, NKJV.
4. *How Thought, Energy & Language Impact Your World* by Elly Molina, published March 26, 2020. © 2020 Thrive Global. Retrieved from https://community.thriveglobal.com/how-thought-energy-language-impact-your-world/#:~:text=Our%20words%20carry%20vibrational%20frequency,words%20co%2Dcreate%20our%20reality on June 15, 2023.
5. See Matthew 12:34.
6. 1 Thessalonians 5:11, NIV, NKJV.
7. See Matthew 5:13-16.
8. See John 10:10.
9. Proverbs 18:21, NKJV.
10. John 14:20, 17:23, Galatians 2:20.
11. See Ephesians 2:6.
12. See Colossians 3:1-3.
13. See Genesis. 1.
14. See Numbers 13:33—where perception informed decision-making.
15. See Matthew 12:34.
16. See 1 John 4:17.
17. Numbers 13:2, NKJV.
18. Numbers 13:32-33, NKJV.
19. See Numbers 14:7-9.
20. See 1 John 4:4.
21. Matthew 4:3, NKJV.
22. Matthew 4:4, NKJV.
23. Mosaic Covenant—Exodus 19:3-6, Noahic Covenant—Genesis 9:8-17; Abrahamic Covenant—Genesis 17:2-5; Davidic Covenant—Acts 13:34-38; Old and New Covenants—Hebrews 8:6-13.
24. See 2 Corinthians 5:17.
25. See Exodus 19:5-6, 1 Peter 2:9, Revelation 5:10.
26. See John 14:12.
27. See Luke 10:19, Ephesians 1:15-22.
28. Genesis 1:28, NKJV.
29. See Matthew 26:36-37.

CHAPTER 4

WHAT IS WORSHIP?

What comes to your mind when you hear the word worship? Does an image of a darkly lit auditorium spring to mind? Are there some musicians on a platform? Spotlights, smoke machines, and other accouterments to "create an atmosphere"? Does it feel like a coffee shop with a "come as you are" and "worship in your own way" vibe? Is the music slow and mellow, with the sound of a ballad echoing as the singer expresses to the Lord how they feel about Him? Or just about how they feel in general?

Something totally different rushes into my mind when I hear the word worship.

When I hear the word worship, I think of sacrifice.

Obedience.

Let me illustrate. There had been ten generations between the lives of Noah and Abram, and Abram likely knew of the Great Flood and God's instructions to Noah. Abram was probably about fifty years old when he encountered the news about the events at the Tower of Babel, where members of his own family intended to defy God and set themselves above. He was raised in a polytheistic family, and his father had household idols for worshiping many gods. The scriptural record is unclear whether Abram served God alone or many gods when the Lord spoke to him, but Abram clearly recognized that this was the voice of Elohim.[1]

"Abram," the Voice said.

Abram stopped in his tracks. None of his father's wooden gods had ever called his name. This Voice was alive. When it spoke, everything in his body quivered in recognition. Awe filled his soul, and without any previous instruction on how to recognize the voice of God, Abram *heard*.

And knew.

"Leave your country, Abram. Leave your family. Leave your father's home," the Voice instructed.

"… and go where?" Abram may have asked.

"Just leave. Go until you arrive at the land I will show you."

Okay, Abram probably thought, *that's a bit vague.* But the Voice was not joking. There was no humor or ambiguity. The Voice was clear and confident. This was a command, a holy invitation; not a suggestion.

WHAT IS WORSHIP?

"I will make you a great nation," the Voice continued, "and I will bless you. I will make your name great, and you will become a blessing."

Abram planted his feet, widening his stance as the weight of these words washed over him, quickening his spirit inside of him, shifting something in his being.

"I will bless everyone who blesses you, and I will curse anyone who curses you," the Voice said, "and through you, Abram, all the people on the earth will be blessed."[2]

That was it. The instructions were not detailed. A timeline was not given. Only a command tied with a promise was all he knew presently, and the next line reads, "So Abram went, as the Lord had told him."[3]

Abram was committed to the voice of the Lord. He governed his life by what God was saying, irrespective of circumstances. He was well established in Haran, all his needs met, but at the prompting of the Voice, he arose and departed Haran, leaving behind the familiarity of his home, his safety, his security, his father, and his inheritance. He set out on a journey filled with uncertainty, without a plan, and even without a destination. His obedience was pure worship. He acknowledged the preeminence of the Voice

> **Abraham's obedience was pure worship—surrendering his all and sacrificing everything to honor God.**

that spoke to him, surrendering his all and sacrificing everything to honor the One who had spoken to him.

This man was so committed to the Lord, choosing to forsake the gods and ideologies of his upbringing for the singular worship of Yahweh, that he is now memorialized as the father of the faith.[4]

In chapter one, we discussed Abraham's journey up the mountain when God told him to sacrifice his son, Isaac. There is no record of Abraham whining or complaining about what God required of him. He *knows* this is the same Voice that brought him out of Haran, that guided his steps and settled him in a land where he prospered and multiplied. This is the same Voice that kept His promise and gave him a son even after Abraham and Sarah had tried to manipulate the fulfillment illegitimately. So up Mount Moriah he climbed with his beloved boy. Laying him down on the altar, with his knife poised, ready to strike, when God intervened.

Abraham had no foreknowledge of how God may intervene amidst this drastic request, but his trust in God was so deep that he was prepared to obey no matter the cost. He demonstrated a sold-out, selfless, steadfast obedience to the voice of God.

Now that is worship.

Bowed down, laid bare, emptied of self, emptied of carnal ambition, and dismissive of any desire for profit, blessing, or reward. Just pure worship. A pure offering of your total being in total surrender.

WHAT IS WORSHIP?

THE LAW OF FIRST MENTION

Many students of the Bible pay attention to what is known as the Law of First Mention. Since we hold that all scripture is God-breathed,[5] even though the words were written down and recorded by people, the author is the Holy Spirit, and the text was written under His divine inspiration.[6] When first introducing a concept, an author goes to great pains to lay the foundation for what they mean when presenting an idea. The meaning of the author's words must be clear at their first mention, or the intent may become increasingly ambiguous as the reader goes along.

In essence, the "first mention" of a word or motif in scripture can be considered a key to understanding the biblical concept and providing a foundation for richer development as the text continues. While not a rigid standard, the Law of the First Mention, both in the literal translation and interpretation of a word and in the contextual application of how it is used, can be a helpful guideline for understanding what God is revealing to us in scripture.

With this in mind, let's consider the first mention of the word *worship* in the Bible. The first time the word worship is used is found in Genesis 22:5. Abraham uses this word to describe to his servants what he is about to do when he gets to the top of Mount Moriah with his son.

Worship.

Shachah in Hebrew.

The THEFT of WORSHIP

At the base of Mount Moriah, Abraham said to his servants, "The boy and I will go over there to *worship—shachah* ..."[7]

Worship here was not in the context of singing or anything musical. Worship here is in the context of a man going up a mountain to give up his most treasured, priceless possession—something—*someone* he loved deeply. And in this act of surrender, offer himself up as "a living sacrifice, holy and acceptable to God, which is your spiritual worship."[8]

The literal translation of *shachah* is to bow down, to prostrate oneself before a superior in homage, before God.[9] The contextual application is radical obedience—laying down your desires, bowing your will, and trusting God to the point of extreme sacrifice in reverent obedience.

This is worship.

ACCEPTABLE WORSHIP

Paul gives instructions about worship in the Book of Romans:

> *"So, here's what I want you to do, God helping you:* ***Take your everyday, ordinary life—your sleeping, eating, going-to-work, and walking around life— and place it before God as an offering.*** *Embracing what God does for you is the best thing you can do for Him. Don't become so well-adjusted to our culture that you fit in without even thinking. Instead, fix your attention on God. You'll be changed from the inside*

WHAT IS WORSHIP?

out. Readily recognize what He wants from you, and quickly respond to it. Unlike the culture around you, always dragging you down to its level of immaturity, God brings out the best of you, and develops well-formed maturity in you."[10]

Another translation begins, "I appeal to you, therefore, brothers, *by the mercies of God* ..."[11] Our motivation to worship, even our very ability to worship, is rooted in the mercies of God. Everything we have comes from Him—from His goodness and mercy—even things we do not deserve.[12] He has given us eternal life,[13] everlasting love,[14] forgiveness,[15] and reconciliation.[16] He has sanctified us,[17] and by Him, we are justified;[18] in Him, we live, move, and have our being.[19] Without Him, we are dead.[20]

Worship requires that we recognize that God is greater than us and that He is the source of life itself—the giver of everything that is good.[21] Our wholehearted acknowledgment of this is grounds for worship.

Worship requires that we recognize that God is greater than us and that He is the source of life itself—the giver of everything that is good.

We place our lives before God as an offering, presenting our bodies as a holy and living sacrifice, giving Him our all. Poured out. Emptied. Bowed down in honor and reverence. All that we have and all that we are belongs to Him, with nothing held back. We give Him total lordship of our mind, our will, and our intellect, and everything within our stewardship is to be managed according to His voice and for His glory. Just as a literal sacrifice was slaughtered and placed on an altar to be burned, we are to place our soul on a spiritual altar to be consumed by the fire of His holy presence.

> *"Therefore, let us be grateful for receiving a kingdom that cannot be shaken, and thus let* **us offer God acceptable worship, with reverence and awe, for our God is a consuming fire**.*"*[22]

Acceptable worship.

That begs the question, if there is acceptable worship, does that mean some worship is not acceptable? Does this not at least give us pause for the common things we hear from our church platforms, "if you feel comfortable," "worship God in your own way," and the general "anything goes" approach as long it is you expressing yourself authentically to God?

Ask Nadab and Abihu, who offered strange fire (their own personal blend of incense) as worship before the Lord, and they were struck down.[23] Ask Uzza, who touched the Ark of the Covenant to steady it—right motives—but was struck dead because his act of worship was unacceptable.[24]

Oh, but that was the Old Testament, right? Surely things have loosened up under the New Covenant.

I wonder what Ananias and Sapphira would say to that?[25] Or the church at Corinth rebuked "for your meetings do more harm than good" as they abused the Lord's Supper.[26]

WHAT IS WORSHIP?

God likes things done His way.

So, what is His way for us to worship? What does acceptable worship look like? What are the boundaries to understanding what kind of worship is acceptable and pleasing to God?

Worship is not an expression of how much we need God or how He makes us feel. It is not our tears of sorrow, though God captures our tears in a bottle and records them in His book.[27] Worship is not coming before Him with a list of petitions and requests for help, though we may do this confidently and boldly.[28]

Worship is something altogether different.

Worship is not an expression of how much we need God or how He makes us feel—worship is something altogether different.

Worship is done for God alone[29] because He is worthy.[30] For His pleasure and glory.[31] In spirit and in truth.[32]

Look again at Paul's words to the Romans:

> *"Don't become so well-adjusted to our culture that you fit in without even thinking."*[33]

To a large degree, the Western church has adopted an incredibly casual approach to worship. The motivation behind the movement has been to remove the barriers of formal liturgy and challenge some invalid traditions[34] that have placed emphasis on our works or that we must first *do* something before we are "cleaned up enough" to come before God.[35] I can appreciate the heart here. Whenever we turn to God, He receives us—even when we come straight from the pig pen with manure stuck to our clothes and hair.[36]

But once we have received the Father's embrace, accepted His sacrifice, and been made a new creation in Christ, we should no longer wallow in the mire and come before Him with the least effort possible to prove He loves us no matter what. This in itself has become a vain, invalid tradition, and too many believers have become so well-adjusted to a contemporary, casual, come-as-you-are church culture that they fit in without thinking.

Believers sip coffee and scroll on mobile devices while being entertained by a professional worship team or joining in on the songs they like. Then they sing words mindlessly while believing they are worshipping the living, breathing, Almighty God whose voice is like thunder that rolls upon many waters and who created the universe from nothing. He is the One who set the stars in the heavens and numbers the grains of sand in the sea, who formed them before they were in their mother's womb and sent His beloved Son to die for their sins so they could enter into blessed union with Him and be seated at His right hand. How can we sing to Him without giving Him our engaged attention? How can we stand before Him without giving Him our all?

What, then, is acceptable worship?

WHAT IS WORSHIP?

To be acceptable to God, our worship must be offered up and given in spirit and in truth. And to worship *in truth*, both our hearts and heads must be engaged in what we are singing and saying and doing. These must *align with who God is* and *who we are in Him*.

To worship in *truth*, both our hearts and heads must be engagaged in what we are singing and saying and doing.

So, with this foundation of understanding what worship is and is not, let's go a little deeper.

ENDNOTES

1. If you are curious, here are two articles to peruse: https://knowingscripture.com/articles/did-abraham-worship-yahweh-before-his-call-in-genesis-12 and https://www.ourancientpaths.org/post/noah-shem-abraham-and-the-tower-of-babel-a-lesson-for-history-lovers both retrieved on June 30, 2023.
2. Author's paraphrase of Genesis 12.
3. Genesis 12:4, NIV.
4. See Romans 4:16, Galatians 3:6-9.
5. See 2 Timothy 3:16-17.
6. See 2 Peter 1:21.
7. Genesis 22:5, CSB.
8. Romans 12:1, ESV.
9. *Shachah* (Hebrew for worship). https://www.biblestudytools.com/lexicons/hebrew/nas/shachah.html. Retrieved on 07/02/2023.
10. Romans 12:1-2, MSG, emphasis added.
11. Romans 12:1, ESV, emphasis added.
12. See Romans 11:36.
13. See John 3:16.
14. See Jeremiah 31:3.
15. See 1 John 1:9.

16. See Romans 5:10-11.
17. See 1 Corinthians 6:11.
18. See Romans 5:9.
19. See Acts 17:28.
20. See Ephesians 2:1.
21. See James 1:17.
22. See Hebrews 12:28-29, ESV emphasis added.
23. See Leviticus 10:1.
24. See 2 Samuel 6:7.
25 See Acts 5:1-11.
26. See 1 Corinthians 1:17-34.
27. See Psalm 56:8.
28. See Hebrews 4:16.
29. See Matthew 4:10.
30. See Revelation 4:11.
31. See Psalm 86:9-10.
32. John 4:24, NASB.
33. Romans 12:1, MSG.
34. See Mark 7:13.
35. See Ephesians 2:8-10.
36. See Luke 15:11-32.

CHAPTER 5

WHEN YOU PRAY

When I pray, I don't read the words to God from some written text. I don't normally open a *book of prayers* and read it aloud as my prayer conversation with the Father. Like you, I pray directly from my spirit—from my belly straight to heaven. I pray from a place of adoration for my Heavenly Father. I pray out of living, vibrant, present fellowship with the Father. I pray from the place of my union with Him in the Spirit.

When you pray, do you open a book or bulletin and recite formal prayers penned by someone else, or do you speak to God openly from your heart?

So, if we don't use other people's words when we pray, why would we do this when we worship? Think about it. So many people regularly sing words to God that are not their own, likely through songs on a screen at a Sunday morning congregation or lyrics from some popular Christian artist as they drive to work. Reciting something someone else wrote and calling it *worship,* isn't it disingenuous? Isn't worship meant to be from the heart? And if "out of the heart, the mouth speaks,"[1] then shouldn't worship, by this definition, infer a necessity of using your own words and not someone else's?

A popular Christian singer may have written a song that was totally valid for them at that place and time in their life—an authentic expression of their relationship and experience, written from *their* heart. If you are in that same place and their words resonate deeply and adequately capture what is also in your heart, then expressing them to God is authentic and intentional. Sing them. But for many songs—most songs—simply borrowing the lyrics verbatim does not authentically represent your heart's expression to God. By extension, if a person is deficient in expressing their own words of adoration to the One they love, carrying no personal overflow from their *own* heart through speech—either in prayer or worship—then evidence suggests that their heart is not healthy because of the absence of personalized, verbalized overflow. For out of the heart, the mouth speaks. If there is nothing original coming out from their own heart by way of their own speech, there is no valid prayer or worship. If there are no personal outflowing words, is their heart weakened, diseased, or even dead?

However, if a person's heart is alive in Christ and if they genuinely love God, they will naturally generate speech to the One they adore—whether it be in prayer or worship. The substitution of their verbalization by using someone else's words while singing weakens, at best, and disqualifies, at worst, their worship because it was not their heart that sourced those words.

If it is out of the heart the mouth speaks, then isn't it also out of the heart, the mouth worships? Worship, in the context of singing, must originate from your own heart; it should consist of *your* own words.

If it is out of the heart the mouth speaks, then isn't it also out of the heart, the mouth worships?

In the summer of 2023, we visited the UK with our friends, Wendy and Todd Walters. Wendy was helping me write this book, and the trip was a great opportunity for her to get to know my heart on the subject. As we sat sipping tea and eating a bacon bap, we discussed how uncommon it is to use other people's words in prayer, yet how routine it is in worship. In fact, few people worship with words from their own hearts; typically, every song they sing is written by others. As we talked, Wendy shared the following illustration that makes the point very well.

> Imagine, for a moment, that you have a dear friend who has just lost her child in a tragic accident. She is deep in grief, wrestling with the conflict in her heart that reaches for God and His goodness, yet grapples with the incomprehensible reality that her child lives no more on this earth.

Sending her "thoughts and prayers" or "good vibes" just doesn't cut it. This is your friend—your covenant friend—the kind of friend with whom you weep when they weep and mourn when they mourn.[2] She is the kind of friend you gladly help bear her burden and thus fulfill the law of Christ.[3]

So, how do you pray for her?

Do you pull out the *Book of Common Prayer* written for the Church of England near the end of the Reformation? Let's pull one from the *Order for Morning Prayer* to send her. That should do it, right?

A PRAYER OF SAINT CHRYSOSTOM

ALMIGHTY God, who hath given us grace at this time with one accord to make our common supplications unto Thee; and do promise that when two or three are gathered together in Thy Name Thou wilt grant their requests. Fulfill now, O Lord, the desires and petitions of Thy servants, as may be most expedient for them; granting us in this world knowledge of Thy truth, and in the world to come life everlasting. Amen.[4]

WHEN YOU PRAY

If you were to write this prayer inside a card and send it to your friend, do you you think she would be comforted in her grief? Probably not.

Well, perhaps a prayer written in the late 1500s is a little too far back. Let's try something a bit more recent. Let's head over to our local Christian bookstore and browse through the card section. This is harder than you thought, isn't it? As you browse through the cards, reading dozens of them, none seem quite right. They are rather generic—none seem to capture the heart and spirit of your friendship or the depth of the burden you carry for her. Still, you read on, finally landing on one with a beautiful nature scene on the front that reads:

> *At your time of loss, I pray you take comfort from all the shared memories of your life with your loved one. Thinking of you in your time of bereavement and sending you lots of love. May God grant you peace and comfort during this difficult season.*

You sign your name and send it off.

The next morning when your friend checks the mailbox, she sees a card from you and brightens at the idea that she was in your thoughts. She opens the envelope expectantly, only to read someone else's pre-printed words. Words from a stranger who does not know her and has never met the child she lost.

The words are hollow.

Instead of bringing her comfort and inviting her into peace, she feels more alone and misunderstood than ever. You signed your name, so you meant for it to be from you, but the message inside is not heartfelt. It is not your authentic expression. It is not in your voice, and it does not sound like the friend she knows. The words are nice, but they are not *yours*.

Maybe the best thing to do is carry your friend in your heart as you go before the throne of God in prayer. Perhaps now is a time to stand in the gap for her, holding her spirit in your spirit as you make intercession for her. Pray authentically from your heart as you help bear her burden in the spirit to lighten hers in the natural.

Your tears flow freely as you commune with the Father and fellowship with Him over your love for her and the great loss she endures. When you are done, you pull out a blank card and write this message:

WHEN YOU PRAY

My friend, I feel your loss profoundly, and I stand with you to help you bear this burden. You are not alone in your grief. You are seen and heard in your sorrow. God is good, even when it doesn't feel that way. He is love. He is life, and He always restores.

Take comfort that God knows everything; even this did not take Him by surprise. Death was not God's will for your son, and though the enemy may have come to steal his life, he is powerless to steal his destiny. God will fulfill all his days in eternity as only God can. It's a mystery beyond our comprehension, but at the restoration of all things, God will restore back to you every moment lost on earth with your son.

I took you before the throne this morning, sat with Father, and wept with Him over you. Jesus was familiar with mourning and knew great loss. In your suffering, I encourage you to lean into the fellowship of His suffering and, from that position, embrace His resurrection power.

May the Holy Spirit alive in you comfort you now, as only He can do. I know that your sorrow will turn to joy in due season, but while you mourn, know that I mourn with you. Receive my love today.

The THEFT *of* WORSHIP

Your words land.

Your friend sobs, but her tears are tears of release. She feels seen. She feels loved. She receives comfort, and her heart takes a step toward healing.

What's the difference?

You didn't try to minister to her with the words of another. You expressed *your heart* in *your own words*, and your friend recognized your spirit contained within them.

"That's brilliant," I told Wendy. Her illustration captures exactly what we are trying to communicate. When we borrow words from someone else, they just do not carry the same heart and spirit. We can get away with this if we are saying them to a stranger. But if we use someone else's words to try to pull off an intimate conversation with a close friend or family member, they know immediately that what we are saying has not been thought up or expressed by us. Disingenuous is the word that keeps coming to mind.

Wendy's example of a prayer in a greeting card demonstrates this well. Personally speaking, If I were to send my wife, Yvonne, a love letter that another man wrote to his wife, she would instantly recognize it. No matter how beautifully that man expressed his feelings for his beloved, or how much I might feel the same way, it would not minister to my wife authentically because I borrowed someone else's expression and tried to pass it off as my own. Even if the man were a gifted poet, and I not so much, my wife naturally would prefer ten words flowing from my own heart than a hundred from someone else.

It is the same with prayer. It is the same with worship.

BACK TO THE WALLS

Remember that Sunday morning during worship when it dawned on me that I could not sing about walls needing to fall down because there were no walls erected between me and the promises of God? The walls had already fallen, so if they were up again, who put them back up? It was certainly not Jesus.

In the song's next line, the writer says, "But You have never failed me …

… *yet.*"

There is a tenure of doubt in that lyric. There is at least the possibility in the writer's mind that God *could* fail him. He just hasn't done so … yet.

What an insult to His faithfulness.

If I were to sing a song to my wife that expressed my gratitude that she has not been unfaithful to me … yet … she would glare at me disapprovingly, and rightfully so. I would never *dream* of verbalizing such nonsense to her. How could I express my love to her by suggesting I had doubts about her faithfulness? How can the "*yet*" be anything less than an insult to the one who has been so consistently faithful to me?

My speech has creative power because I am made in the image of God. Therefore, I must be careful not to undo the finished work of Christ with my mouth.

I contend that the carelessness of people's speech and their singing is one major reason why the Church has no power. In the context of my meditation on the power and importance of the words I speak, I received a direct *rhema* from the Lord. When He spoke to me, I captured His words as best as I could, and that is when He gave me the mandate to write this book and gave me the title, *The Theft of Worship*.

> **The carelessness of people's speech and their singing is one major reason why the Church has no power.**

What follows came straight from the Father to my spirit. The voice in the following text is partially from heaven's vantage point and some through my own lens in order to verbalize it in English. I was in the Spirit when this came to me, and here it is verbatim:

> *When we pray, we rarely use someone else's words, nor should we. Because how can another know accurately what is in our hearts that needs to be expressed to God? Similarly, when it comes to our worship, how can the words of another intermediary knowingly and sufficiently express our love for God?*

Love is very personal, and worship is an expression of our love for God. How can this be verbalized by someone else? Surely, this is totally inappropriate.

> *"Many Christians think that they are worshipping Me, God, not knowing that they are using an intermediary that I have not authorized in your life or the life of other worshippers. Anyone that mediates between Me (God) and man is occupying the role of a priest. Now that we're in the New Covenant, there is no place for a priest since believers are, themselves, a royal priesthood. Any such intermediary—other people's words—is illegal and not authorized by Me."*

Satan has always wanted to steal worship and bring glory unto himself. Obviously, Christians will not worship him, but to a large degree, the enemy has hijacked Christian worship by interjecting well-meaning, well-intentioned worship leaders and songwriters who are writing songs that are very valid and appropriate for themselves but may not be appropriate and valid for another. Not bad songs in and of themselves, but probably inappropriate for another to embrace and sing along glibly without deliberately reading the words and determining if they are accurately reflective of the heart of the worshipper.

We are to sing our own songs directly to God. There is no place for a priest other than the High Priest, Himself.[5] *Singing the songs of another is not God's ideal intention. He wants to hear our own song from the heart. This is giving God our very best. In the Western Church today, there are probably more songs being recorded and sung by others than at any time in history, and at the same time, the Western Church is probably more devoid of supernatural power than it has ever seen.*

Jesus has not changed, but maybe our understanding of worship has. It's time to sing our own words from our own heart, for true worshipers are those that will worship Him in Spirit and truth.

Later, as I meditated further and prayed in the Spirit, I heard God say, "Paul, because I am in you and you are in Me, you can only say what I can say. If I can't say it, neither can you." I took His words to heart, and it has become the measuring stick by which I evaluate every word that proceeds from my mouth—no matter the occasion. As I began sharing this revelation with my friends and family, I got more insight regarding using my words versus the words of another when speaking to God. For example, the Anglican *Book of Common Prayer* contains many good prayers, the recitation of which brings me back to my childhood years as I sat in parochial school assembly each morning. I enjoy reading through these occasionally. I can open it and read a prayer for the day, and it is a perfectly good prayer, and it can inspire my meditation. But when I pray, I do not pick up this book and read it to the Father. That isn't how I pray. Reading someone else's prayer is good, but there is better.

And I choose better.

WE ARE ONE

When I became born again and was filled with the Spirit, I entered into union with the Trinity.[6] Christ in me, the hope of glory became a reality.[7] It is no longer I who live, but Christ who lives in me.[8] And because Christ and the Father are one, and I am in Christ, then I and the Father are also one.[9]

Because of this oneness, I don't cry out to a God who is distant and far off somewhere in the heavens. I don't cry out, "Lord, I need you," because I have Him. I often use the pronouns "us" and "we" in my language. When I speak or sing this way, it rehearses the reality of my oneness with the Trinity—Father, Son, Holy Spirit … and Paul. *We* are one.

This is the meditation of my heart, and it is intertwined around every fiber of my being, so I never feel alone. You can drop me anywhere on this planet, and I will not feel alone. I am at peace everywhere I go because They—the Triune God—are with me, and we are together.

The THEFT *of* WORSHIP

When I pray, I say things like, "What are *we* going to do today? What exploits shall *we* perform?" Even when I am singing songs to the Lord, I often sing, "*We* are good, *we* are great," as I acknowledge that I am one with God.[10] I realize that speaking this way may seem odd to most people. It just isn't how we have been brought up within evangelicalism, yet the weight of scripture screams of our unity with Him and the new nature, the God-in-you-now, divine nature. It is no longer I that liveth but Christ liveth in me.[11] He that is joined to the Lord is one spirit.[12] Using this terminology around the Godhead can even create a cognitive dissonance that throws up warning signs that speaking this way approaches arrogance at best and narcissism at worst. I can assure you the theology is sound.

Father, Son, and Holy Spirit are unique and individual but one.[13] "There is one body and one Spirit—one Lord, one faith, one baptism; one God and Father of all who is above all, and through all and in you all."[14] You are one with Christ. Christ is one with the Father. Therefore, you are one with the Father, who is one with Jesus, who is one with the Holy Spirit. You are one with God. To further prove the point, even the apostle Paul admonishes the church in Corinth for being carnal and behaving like mere men.[15]

> **Any time that your words do not agree with God, you create friction in your spirit.**

Any time that your words do not agree with God, you create friction in your spirit. You are seated in heavenly places at the right hand of the Father,[16] and you have been given all authority in heaven and earth through Jesus.[17] You are part of the finished work of Christ—the New Covenant fulfilled,[18] and you have no reason to undo that work with the confession of your mouth. Any time you do, you feel the tension because you step out of unity, and the power to live victoriously as an overcomer evaporates.

The more you embrace that you are one with Christ, the less you are willing to release careless words into the atmosphere. This understanding is fundamental to your effectiveness and directly links to your experience as a believer living an abundant life.

THE PRIESTHOOD OF THE BELIEVER

"For there is one God and one mediator between God and mankind, the man Jesus Christ."[19] As believers under the New Covenant, through Jesus, we have been granted direct access to the Father by His Spirit.[20] Jesus is our High Priest, and He fulfilled the priestly role once and for all through His death and resurrection.[21] He is the final mediator between us and the Father. Because we are in Christ, we share in this priestly status. We do not require a priest as an intermediate for the presence of God or as a go-between for us to receive His forgiveness.

As Christians, we have the authority to read, interpret, and apply God's Word to our lives. We cannot push that responsibility onto a pastor or priest. We have the privilege to come boldly before the throne of grace, where we will obtain mercy and find grace.[22] Jesus said we could ask Him (directly) for anything in His name, and He will do it to glorify the Father.[23] We are members of God's household—His family,[24] and God desires us to communicate directly with Him in the same way we desire our children to speak directly with us.

Would you prefer your child to have a friend write down everything they should say to you? Of course not. You want your children to converse with you in their own words, from their own mind, expressing their feelings and understanding at whatever level of maturity or stage of growth they are in.

If you are reading or singing someone else's words, this could be like having a priest between you and God—someone to facilitate your expression. If you are singing other people's lyrics, is it possible you are inserting an unauthorized priest between you and the lover of your soul?

PRAY WITHOUT CEASING

As a new believer, when I first read Paul's words to the Thessalonians to "pray without ceasing,"[25] I got nervous. I thought this meant I needed to pray at every coffee break and get up an hour early to pray before I started my day. At that time, I lived a more compartmentalized life, and my prayers were offered only during specific prayer times. I saw absolutely no way I could pray without ceasing. How could I possibly get anything else done?

Of course, that is not at all what Paul meant. Let's look at this passage in *The Passion Translation* for a new lens through which to look:

> "*Let joy be your continual feast.* **Make your life a prayer.** *And in the midst of everything, be always giving thanks, for this is God's perfect plan for you in Christ Jesus.*"[26]

"Make your life a prayer." Okay, I can really get behind that.

I am in constant communion with the Father. And once I received the baptism of the Holy Spirit, and I experienced and experimented with praying in tongues, praying without ceasing was no longer an unobtainable task. Because I am aware of the God-self inside of me, I am constantly convening. I am walking in assembly with the Godhead 24/7. In every activity I engage in, They are with me. I pray regularly in English, but because I am a spirit and I have been filled by God's Spirit, I communicate continuously with God in the Spirit as I pray in tongues. Since I have been born again, born of the Spirit, my native language is now tongues.

Speaking in tongues is spirit language because once born of the Spirit, this is my new nature. The degree to which you speak your new language of the Spirit is the degree to which you will identify

> **The degree to which you speak your new language of the Spirit is the degree to which you will identify and live in the new world your speech is creating.**

and live in the new world your speech is creating. If you only speak a physical language, be it English, French, Spanish, etc., that's the world you will be aware of. But as you increase in speaking in the Spirit—communing with the Trinity in their native tongue—you will become increasingly aware of the spirit world for which you were created. So I can be at work, driving, sending out emails, and still be praying in the Spirit because it is not my mind that is engaged—it is my spirit. It is freedom at its finest. It is a taste of heaven on earth.

My spirit is always on. Always engaged. Always plugged in. Always receiving and always in communion with the Trinity.

It would be impossible to pray without ceasing if I were attempting to do this by reciting the words of another. My spirit must be involved. Alert. Yielded. Participating.

EXPRESSING LOVE FOR GOD

Before we leave the topic of prayer, let me share an illustration from my friend, Dr. Kerry Wood.

> Think of a young couple in love. They have been courting one another long distance. The young man is from California, and the young woman is from Massachusetts. Throughout the courtship, they have sent each other beautiful love letters, expressing their heart, revealing things about themselves, and getting to know one another better.

WHEN YOU PRAY

At last, the wedding day arrives. The couple is no longer far from each other, the wedding ceremony has ended, and they join one another in the honeymoon suite. Only instead of looking into each other's eyes, kissing, and enjoying the freedom and beauty of intimacy, he sits on the balcony reading her letters to him, and she sits in the bridal chamber reading his letters to her.

That is so weird. It is their wedding night. Vows have been said, and they are free to experience each other—not just read about each other—but to talk direct to each other and even to undress each other and enjoy a greater revelation … The bride and groom can now be one. They should no longer be content to only read about each other; it is time to *know* each other–intimately.

It is a theological or communicative error where the church at large has this notion that God is off in the heavens and you are here on earth, separated from Him by time and space. When you know that Christ is in you, it is very odd to be speaking about Him at a distance. You are in His chamber—look Him in the eyes and express your love directly to Him.

Telling others about Him is wonderful, and we should do that. Speaking or singing about Him and His greatness or His other attributes is delightful. This is offering praise, and there is a place for praise. It is good and pleases Him immensely, but you must also remember that He is right there inside of you, and to worship Him is intimate communication from your heart to His.

Think of worship in the context of expressing your love to God directly. It is a demonstration of your gratitude—heart-to-heart, eyeball-to-eyeball, a holy embrace—innocent, pure, and intimate. It is a celebration of your union.

> **Worship is a demonstration of your gratitude—heart-to-heart, eyeball-to-eyeball, a holy embrace—innocent, pure, and intimate.**

Just as the Father, Son, and Holy Spirit have unique identities, personalities, and functions, you also have a unique identity and personality that is yours. Your personhood does not get lost inside the Trinity. Your expression of your personhood is distinct, but you are one together with Him. "He that is joined to the Lord is one Spirit with Him."[27]

I have this flat-on-the-floor awe and reverence response to God. I fully enter the mystery that I—a once-flawed, imperfect human being—now have access to and am in oneness with the Perfect One. It boggles my mind. It is a mystery—a capital "M" Mystery—a paradox I embrace by faith as my understanding expands to greater capacity. In my belly, I am so in awe and so fearful of this wonderful, terrible God, and at the same time, I approach Him with the confidence and innocence of a child coming to their parent in total trust. That God has chosen, in the person of Jesus, to be connected to *me* is beyond my comprehension and a joy and delight to my soul.

The THEFT *of* WORSHIP

ENDNOTES

1. See Matthew 12:34-40.
2. See Romans 12:15.
3. See Galatians 6:2.
4. *The Book of Common Prayer,* 1549. Public Domain.
5. See Hebrews 4:14-16.
6. See Romans 6:1-7, 1 Corinthians 6:17, 2 Corinthians 5:21
7. See Colossians 1:24-27.
8. See Galatians 2:20.
9. See John 10:30.
10. See John 17:22.
11. Galatians 2:20, KJV.
12. 1 Corinthians 6:17, KJV.
13. See 1 John 5:6-8.
14. See Ephesians 4:4.
15. 1 Corinthians 3:3, NKJV.
16. See Matthew 22:44, Acts 2:33.
17. See Matthew 28:18-20.
18. See John 17:4.
19. See 1 Timothy 2:5.
20. See Ephesians 2:18.
21. See Hebrews 4:14.
22. See Hebrews 4:16.
23. See John 14:13-14.
24. See Ephesians 2:19.
25. See 1 Thessalonians 5:17.
26. 1 Thessalonians 5:16-18, TPT.
27. 1 Corinthians 6:17, NKJV.

CHAPTER 6

THE SUPERNATURAL ON-RAMP

My parents took me and my siblings to Sunday School at the Assemblies of God church near our home in Derbyshire, England. Through the effort of a traveling evangelistic group, I became born again at the tender age of six. I grew up in the local church community, and my Christian faith became an integral part of my development. I learned to sing hymns and spiritual songs. I learned how to pray and how to believe God for healing and deliverance. My faith was not a separate Sunday morning experience but an everyday reality.

Years later, as a new immigrant in Canada, I further pressed in to read the Bible more faithfully as a Christian. I fervently started believing the Bible at this point, and the Lord began challenging me. I read, "But seek first the kingdom of God and His righteousness, and all these things shall be added to you."[1] As I later leveled up and took God at His Word to seek Him first, I began to experience "all these things" as He had promised them to me.

I'm grateful for this foundation. Believing the Word of God is true and applying it to my life had me on fire for God. I earnestly sought the Lord, and I hearkened to His voice. He was alive in me.

Shortly thereafter, on September 28, 1997, to be specific, I was in my front living room with my friend, Peter. Late that night, we were praising God together. I was saying things like, "Lord, You are good. Lord, You are great. Lord, You are amazing … fantastic … incredible … stupendous … omnipotent … omniscient … omnipresent … omni-I'm-running-out-of-adjectives, but my heart is filled with Your praises."

My vocabulary was simply not adequate to contain my expression of gratitude, adoration, and praise to God. I was out of words and almost frustrated with how repetitive my prayer was when Peter encouraged me, "Paul, stop speaking in English. Let the Holy Spirit baptize you. Let Him fill you with power and ask Him to fill your mouth with the gift of tongues."

Now, growing up in an AG church, baptism in the Holy Ghost was not a new concept for me, but I had never reached to unwrap the gift. That night, I did.

The moment my heart opened to receive this gift, I spoke in faith and began speaking in tongues. It flowed from my belly like a river. I had exhausted my vocabulary in English, but out of my spirit, I was able to articulate endless words of unlimited exaltation to the One whom I adored. Where before I was restricted by the languages of men, now, I had a never-ending, always-renewing, perfect, pure, and present vocabulary to communicate from my spirit to God's Spirit. It was incredible, and Peter and I prayed in the Holy Ghost for hours. We took a break for a cup of tea and continued praying non-stop until 6:30 in the morning.

When Peter saw the time, he realized he would need to get ready for work soon and said, "Paul, we had better stop and get some sleep."

I went to bed full of joy and slept for just thirty minutes before my alarm went off at 7:00 am. I should have been tired. I should have been dragging my feet and needing a strong cup of tea to get going, but I felt as though I had twelve full hours of restful sleep. It was incredible.

It was supernatural.

And it was just the beginning. That September night in 1997 marked a shift in my intimacy with the Father, as well as an increase of faith, power, and practice in my life. One encounter opened up a whole new world of possibilities for life in the Spirit. I discovered that the baptism of the Holy Spirit is the supernatural on-ramp to living life more abundantly.

> **One encounter opened up a whole new world of possibilities for life in the Spirit.**

INSTANT UPGRADE

I could not contain my enthusiasm and joy over exploring the gift of the Holy Ghost. I was exhilarated by and through the Holy Spirit. I had been aware of this doctrine but had not yet experienced the power of its reality. I returned to the church that I had been attending. Doctrinally, it was Baptist, but when I shared my experience with my friends, three of them received the baptism of the Holy Spirit and spoke in tongues shortly thereafter. Many lives were impacted, and many of us began seeing God move in tangible ways.

After I was baptized in the Holy Spirit, the Bible instantly became alive to me in a way it had never been before. Before when I read it, I would understand it; but now, when I read it, things jumped off the page and grabbed my attention. Scripture began to embody His presence—as though physically tangible. The Word became alive; that's the only way I know how to describe it.

For the first time in my life, I was receiving *Rhema*—a timely, personal, valuable, supernatural utterance from Father to my heart. And this didn't happen just when I read the Bible. As I went about my normal life and responsibilities, I would also receive downloads from the Spirit of God. My life in the Spirit had begun. I began to be able to see in the Spirit—identifying things that could not naturally be seen and perceiving things that could not naturally be understood based on the data available. I began hearing things that could only be picked up in the Spirit. I was able to understand circumstances supernaturally. There was no other explanation for what was happening to me other than the baptism of the Holy Spirit.

My trade at the time was buying and selling cars. Before life in the Spirit, if someone called me about a car, I would automatically make an appointment to meet with them. Now, my senses became more sharpened—my spiritual senses had been awakened. So, when a prospective client would call, as I was in conversation with them, I would know in my belly, "Don't make this appointment. Don't waste your time," or conversely, "This person will buy from you." I would just know things in my spirit. I'm not negating my natural intuition and experience as a businessman, but something was different. I had such a heightened sense of knowing people and hearing God's voice that I became laser-focused on how I spent my time. For example, in the business world, when I had a car for sale, I needed only one good, qualified buyer—not ten. I didn't need to waste time, energy, or resources on nine non-producing appointments, and the Holy Spirit directed my efforts. My profit and productivity went up measurably.

In fact, I am married to my beautiful wife, Yvonne, today as a direct result of my baptism in the Holy Spirit. As I became activated by the things of the Spirit, I opened my home, leading Bible studies and a youth group from my living room, and often ended up cooking for them all at least one night a week. Yvonne had been attending the same Pentecostal church where I had now migrated to, and her attraction to me was the attraction of the Holy Spirit in me—I was a young man who loved the Lord, and it made me whole. It made me confident. Yvonne saw my heart for God and was attracted to my boldness in Christ and my confidence in life, both fruits of the Spirit alive in me. We married in August 1999.

By the Summer of 2000, we were expecting and happily on our way to New England, where I was enrolled in Zion Bible College. While there, my relationship with the Holy Spirit became increasingly practical. Yvonne was working full-time, and in the following years, we had two small children. I was a full-time student and heavily involved in ministry, so time was precious. I was in the United States on a student visa and had no work permit, so generating income was a challenge.

Thankfully, I always had a knack for buying and selling. This natural talent, along with the favor of God, enabled us to pay our way through Bible college. Moreover, Yvonne was also experiencing the combination of God's favor upon her diligence and career-banking experience. Our success was supernatural. God's provision through that season was highlighted to us, and it continues to this day. Every single pursuit we have put our hands to accomplish was and continues to be touched by God's supernatural power—all as a result of life in the Spirit.

> **Every single pursuit we have put our hands to accomplish was and continues to be touched by God's supernatural power—all as a result of life in the Spirit.**

THE SUPERNATURAL ON-RAMP

HOLY GHOST 101

You may be wondering why I put this chapter about the Holy Spirit in a book about the *theft of worship*. The reason is that *baptism in the Spirit* with the gift of *speaking* and therefore *singing* in tongues is essential to God's Spirit communing with your spirit and your spirit communing with His.

> **"God is Spirit,** *and those who worship Him must* **worship in spirit** *and truth."*[2]

Your spirit doesn't speak English; your soul does. Your mind requires language and understanding to speak to God in your native tongue—and this is a wonderful thing. But there is more.

God is Spirit, and He speaks Spirit—in whispers,[3] in groanings that cannot be uttered,[4] and He breathes life into us by His Spirit.[5] To worship God in spirit (from our spirit) requires worshipping Him with the part of us that is engaged with the mysteries of God.[6] Paul said it like this:

> *"For he who speaks in a tongue does not speak to men but to God, for no one understands him; however, in the Spirit,* **he speaks mysteries."**[7]

Another translation says it this way:

> *"Give yourselves to the gifts God gives you. Most of all, try to proclaim His truth. If you praise Him in the private language of tongues, God understands you, but no one else does, for* **you are sharing intimacies just between you and Him."**[8]

Speaking in tongues is how we communicate intimately with God. It is a language no one has ever cursed in, said anything stupid or cruel in, or perverted in any way. It is a language from your spirit only God can understand. Even the enemy cannot overhear your prayers when you pray in tongues or mess with your mind as you worship in the Spirit.

Chances are, if you have read this far, you are either already baptized in the Holy Ghost, or your heart is open to it, and you are hungry for more. Either way, I pray this chapter provokes you to explore this gift further and dive in with both feet.

When you got saved, salvation was the whole package. God the Father, Jesus the Son, and the Holy Spirit all came to live in your heart, and your union with Them began. It was complete from day one. So, baptism in the Holy Spirit is not about salvation—it is about empowerment.

> **Baptism in the Holy Spirit is not about salvation—it is about empowerment.**

Baptism in the Holy Spirit grants you power.[9] Life in the Spirit is how we overcome the lusts of the flesh. It allows us to be led supernaturally and exhibit the fruit of the Spirit in our lives. Being baptized in the Holy Ghost is the supernatural on-ramp to being an overcomer and living victoriously.[10] All your rights and privileges as a believer and as a child of God are available to you right there for you to access 24/7. The Holy Spirit plugs you into the power of God and allows you to become who He created you to be before the foundations of the earth.

THE SUPERNATURAL ON-RAMP

TRY IT—YOU'LL LIKE IT!

There is no sweeter worship available to you than praying and singing in the Holy Ghost. And when you are in a corporate setting, and you find that the words of the songs being sung do not align with the Spirit of God in you or agree with His promises for you, then you have access to this beautiful language where you cannot speak out of alignment. It is pure, and perfect, and protected. But before I can invite you to adjust your practice of worship, I must invite you to experience the baptism of the Holy Spirit and exercise the gift of tongues.

If you have never received this wonderful gift, we invite you to do so now. The baptism of the Holy Spirit is God's intention for you as a born-again believer. Jesus said:

> *"And I will pray the Father, and He will give you another Helper, that He may abide with you forever—the Spirit of truth,* **whom the world cannot receive** *because it neither sees Him nor knows Him;* **but you know Him for He dwells with you and will be in you.**"[11]

You need to understand that this baptism is separate—an additional outpouring not automatically received at the time of salvation.

> *"Now when the apostles who were at Jerusalem heard that Samaria had received the word of God, they sent Peter and John to them, who when they had come down* **prayed for them that they might receive the Holy Spirit. For as yet, He had fallen upon none of them.**

They had only been baptized in the name of the Lord Jesus."[12]

You must believe in order to receive the gift. Peter said:

*"Repent, and let every one of you be baptized in the name of Jesus Christ for the remission of sins; an*d **you shall receive the gift of the Holy Spirit.**"[13]

It is received by faith. You might feel something, or you might not. Your feelings are not the evidence of receiving the gift—*power* is the evidence. We "receive the promise of the Spirit through faith."[14] Paul reminded the Galatians of this when he asked:

"Did you receive the Spirit by the works of the law, or **by the hearing of faith?**"[15]

When you got saved, you believed in your heart, confessed with your mouth, and received Christ into your spirit.[16] When you receive the baptism of the Holy Spirit, you are to believe in your heart and ask for the gift. God will give you the Holy Spirit when you ask Him. He's a good Father. Jesus said it like this:

"If you then, being evil, know how to give good gifts to your children, how much more will your heavenly **Father give the Holy Spirit to those who ask Him!**"[17]

In the book of Acts, each time it records people being filled with the Holy Spirit, they also speak in tongues.[18]

THE SUPERNATURAL ON-RAMP

*"And they **were all filled** with the Holy Spirit and **began to speak with other tongues**, as the Spirit gave them utterance."*[19]

Notice that the believers did the speaking. The Holy Spirit did not take over their mouth and force syllables to come out. God's Spirit gave utterance to their spirits, and they responded by opening their mouths and releasing the gift. It takes faith and obedience to speak in tongues.

Later, when Paul speaks of his own experience, he clarifies that his will is involved. Notice as he repeats "I will" again and again:

*"For if I pray in a tongue, my spirit prays, but my understanding is unfruitful. What is the conclusion, then? **I will pray** with the spirit, and **I will also pray** with the understanding. **I will sing** with the spirit, and **I will also sing** with the understanding."*[20]

Much of the Church is fixated upon singing with understanding, but scripture encourages us to go beyond that and have us sing in the Spirit—singing in tongues.

I pray in tongues—a lot. I sing in tongues—a lot. I know many who have received the baptism pray in the Spirit occasionally, softly under their breath now and again, but I just push it and push it and push it—then I push it a little bit more. I do this because I have learned that if I use the gift in a minimalist way, my results are minimalistic. But when I exercise this gift with liberality, my results are gigantic.

Scripture tells us that He who prays in an unknown tongue edifies himself.[21] To edify means to build in a literal sense.[22] When you pray in tongues, you build yourself up—you increase your spiritual capacity to contain the increasing revelation of God in your spirit. Praying in the Holy Ghost expands you on the inside. It is supernatural. The more you build yourself up, the more capacity you have. The more capacity you have, the more you re-present Jesus on the earth. If there is anything in your life that you need to push for—push for this—pray in the Spirit.

> **Praying in the Holy Ghost expands you on the inside, increasing your spiritual capacity to contain the increasing revelation of God in your spirit.**

Sing in the spirit.

Live in the Spirit.

Be in the Spirit.

It will expand your awareness of your God-nature 24/7. It will fill you with the mysteries of God, and as you operate regularly in the supernatural realm, you embrace further revelation and wisdom and knowledge of heaven and pull it into the natural realm. Your life will change exponentially.

Tongues is a limitless language to converse with a limitless God. Go ahead and experience this incredible gift. Let it become natural and normal in your life. Let it become like breathing. Your physical body needs air in order to live. Your spirit is no

THE SUPERNATURAL ON-RAMP

different. It requires the *pneuma* or the *ruach*—the breath of God—in order for it to live. Without His breath, we're just dust on the ground.[23]

Your spirit must breathe God's Spirit; otherwise, you are only living in the flesh.

> *"The mind governed by the flesh is death, but the mind governed by the Spirit is life and peace."*[24]

Being led by the Spirit is your validation as a child of God.

> *"For those who are led by the Spirit of God are the children of God."*[25]

Don't wait one more minute. Pray in the Spirit. Sing in the Spirit. Be led of the Spirit.

The THEFT *of* WORSHIP

ENDNOTES

1. Matthew 6:33, NKJV.
2. John 4:24, NIV.
3. See 1 Kings 19:11-13.
4. See Romans 8:26.
5. See Genesis 2:6-7, John 20:21-22.
6. See Job 11:7, Daniel 2:28, Matthew 13:11, Romans 16:25, 1 Corinthians 1:26, Ephesians 3:9, 1 Timothy 3:16, Revelation 10:7.
7. 1 Corinthians 14:2, NKJV, emphasis added.
8. 1 Corinthians 14:1-2, MSG, emphasis added.
9. See Acts 1:8
10. See Galatians 5:16-25.
11. John 14:16-17, NKJV, emphasis added.
12. Acts 8:14-16, NKJV, emphasis added.
13. Acts 2:38, NKJV, emphasis added.
14. Galatians 3:14, NKJV.
15. Galatians 3:2, NKJV, emphasis added.
16. See Romans 10:9.
17. Luke 11:13, NKJV, emphasis added.
18. See Acts 2:4, 10:44-46, 19:6-7.
19. Acts 2:4, NKJV, emphasis added.
20. See 1 Corinthians 14:14-15.
21. See 1 Corinthians 14:4.
22. Edify. *Webster's 1828 Dictionary*. Retrieved from www.webstersdictionary1828.com on July 21, 2023.
23. SeeGenesis 2:7, Psalm 103:14.
24. Romans 8:6, NIV.
25. Romans 8:14, NIV.

CHAPTER 7

TO ILLUSTRATE

Our words matter whether thought, spoken, or sung. If we agree on this point, then providing some examples of popular lyrics that do not align with what Jesus would sing might prove helpful. In this chapter, I will share a few phrases commonly used in contemporary songs that illustrate the kind of situation that puts our words at odds with our beliefs. At first glance, these may seem harmless, but if you look more closely, you will find that these lyrics are contrary to sound doctrine. This contradiction is reason enough to pause and reflect on what we are singing and why.

I will ask you to picture the following scenario with me to set the stage. Imagine I am standing before you wearing a blue shirt and singing, "Oh Lord, I need a blue shirt. I long for a blue shirt. I ask for the presence of a blue shirt here in this place. I want it. I need it. I'm desperate for it. It is my heart's desire. I earnestly yearn for a collared, button-down, long-sleeve, blue shirt. Oh God, how I need a blue shirt."

"Paul," God says, "you already have a blue shirt, son. You are wearing it. I have already given it to you."

"Oh yes!" I say, looking down. "That's true. I already have a blue shirt—and not just any blue shirt, but the exact one I asked You for. I must sound silly standing here singing out a request for something I already possess."

LORD, I NEED YOU

My example of asking for a blue shirt I already have is hyperbole, of course, but this same scenario plays out in auditoriums all around the world with astounding regularity. Believers stand with their hands in the air or over their hearts and earnestly sing, "God, I need You. Oh, how I need You …"

But they already have Him. He lives within them. They are in union with Him, so in a practical sense, how can they need what they already have?

Think about it. If you are born again, if you are born of the Spirit, you already have all of God. How can you say or sing that you need Him or need more of Him? You don't need something that you already have. It is a deception of the enemy to have people looking for and chasing after what they've already got. It downgrades their belief system. It dilutes their theology, therefore, weakening their authority as believers.

TO ILLUSTRATE

Jesus said, "Lo, I am with you always [remaining with you perpetually—regardless of circumstance, and on every occasion], even to the end of the age."[1] The Bible tells us again and again that God is with us, that He will never leave us or forsake us,[2] and that there is nowhere we can run from His presence—no place we can hide from Him.[3] He fills the heavens and the earth, and He is everywhere.[4] We have God always and without fail.[5] He is our present help in time of need.[6] He dwells among us.[7] We can boldly approach Him.[8] In Him we live, move, and have our being.[9] None of these are questionable doctrines or grey areas open for interpretation.

God is with us. Always.[10]

I have Him. He has me, and we are one. I don't need Him because it is no longer I who lives, but Christ who lives in me.[11] So, I already have Him—and so do you. If you say, "God, I need You," you are denying your position in Christ. We have already agreed that words create worlds—our words create our world—so the recitation of these words can put us positionally outside of the New Covenant.

The recitation of words that are theologically in error can put us positionally outside of the New Covenant.

Which covenant are you under? Do you want to go back to offering sacrifices of bulls and goats before you can approach God? Or have you received the once-and-for-all sacrifice of

Jesus, who has reconciled you to the Father and come to dwell permanently in your heart? I encourage you not to undo with your mouth what Jesus has done for you with His blood.

Let's look at another one we hear often …

WE WELCOME YOU IN THIS PLACE

Many corporate gatherings kick off with prayers or songs that invite or welcome God's presence into the meeting. You will hear things like, "Lord, we welcome You into this place." But He is already there because you are there, and He is in you. And if you've gathered two or three of you, His presence is guaranteed.[12]

When you are in your home with your family, all seated around the table together, do you say to your spouse, "Darling, I wish to welcome you into this place today"? That would be odd, wouldn't it? Of course, she is welcome; she lives there. Your home is her dwelling place. Her name is on the deed.

Under the Old Covenant, the Lord's dwelling place was in a glory cloud, or tabernacle, or temple. You could approach and say, "The Lord is in this place." But under the New Covenant, the Lord is everywhere. He is present even in a consecrated space such as an auditorium or a room people call a sanctuary. You may call it what you like, but even a consecrated room is just a room. *You* are the sanctuary. *We* are the sanctuary. The place where we congregate as believers to meet and worship the Lord is just a place, whatever we call it.

If the Spirit of God lives inside you, you are a holy place. You can never leave the holy place. Why would we want to create holy and unholy places with our speech?

We must not allow our words to be careless or cheap. We don't want the octane of our authority diluted by bad theology or erroneous confessions. I am careful never to undo my position in Christ or water down the power of God inside me by my own mouth.

This "undoing" of our position in Christ is not limited just to words we say or sing. Sometimes, it is due to an error in our thinking, a belief that has been adopted because it is mainstream rather than because it represents truth. Let me provide you with an example of what I mean.

LEAD ME INTO HIS PRESENCE— MORE OF HIS PRESENCE

You and I cannot be led into God's presence because we are already there. There is little wonder that gatherings struggle to find unity or manifest God's presence. Why? Because they are waiting on a worship leader to usher them somewhere they already are, or because they are looking for Him in the clouds or the *altar*, waiting to *feel* something to reassure them that He is there.

I'm not saying that God does not manifest Himself tangibly at times. The presence of the Lord can sometimes grow weighty, and when people are gathered in unity, there are times when

God manifests in undeniable signs, wonders, and miracles. Even this is not "more" of His presence; it is a unique expression or manifestation of His presence for His pleasure and purpose.

I am present with my wife when we are sitting and talking as much as I am present with her when we are in the ecstasy of intimacy. I am present with her when I bring her a cup of coffee as much as I am present with her when I plan an elaborate, extravagant evening to bestow diamonds and rubies and pearls upon her. The manifestations of my love may have degrees of tangible expression, but my presence with her and my love for her is constant throughout.

My wife, Yvonne, cannot have any more of me when we are in union together. Only if we are separated by time or space does she long for me, need, or want more of me. When I am with her, holding her in my arms, looking her in the eye, and speaking with her, how strange it would be to hear her say, "Paul, I want more of your presence?"

In the same way, if you are saying, "God, I want more of Your presence," with your own words, you have separated yourself from His presence. How can you ask for more of what you already have?

At best, this is an issue of an awareness of God's presence. At worst, it is an insult to what He has provided for us and told us about in His Word. Bad speech can betray your theology.

Jesus went to the cross to reconcile us to the Father. He released His Spirit on the earth and made us flesh containers of His

Spirit. He endured the crucifixion, ascended to the Father, and sent His Holy Spirit to indwell each of us. We embody His presence—His Spirit. If we live *for* Jesus, there is a separation; but if we live *as* Jesus, though we are not Jesus, we re-present Him on the earth.

If we live *for* Jesus, there is a separation; but if we live *as* Jesus, though we are not Jesus, we re-present Him on the earth.

We don't live *for* Jesus; we live *as* Jesus.

We don't speak *for* Jesus; we speak *as* Jesus.

Or at least we should be living this way because "as He is, so are we in this world."[13] When I stand before you, you shouldn't just be seeing me; you should be seeing a version of Jesus called Paul. Like Jesus, I am meant to do only what I see the Father doing.[14] I have been created for good works God prepared in advance for me to do.[15] He is delighted when I obey His voice.[16] He gave me dominion over the earth.[17] So I don't need to beseech Him to move; I just need to partner with what He is already doing. This brings me to another common error often sung.

HOLY SPIRIT, COME

How many songs have you heard that ask the Holy Spirit to come? Quite a few, I imagine. But asking Him to come is truly strange if you think about it. Isn't He already here? The Holy Spirit is present; He is waiting for our obedience. We are not waiting on Him; He is waiting on us.

When we agree with God, His empowerment comes on the earth. The Triune God—Father, Son, and Holy Spirit—are alive and at work inside us, so wherever we are, He is. Asking Him to come is like holding your child in your lap and asking them to come to you as if they were across the room.

HOLY SPIRIT, MOVE—HAVE YOUR WAY

When I hear people say to God, "Have Your way, Lord," I almost shake my head because the only thing blocking Him having His way is human cooperation. So, someone saying, "Have Your way" to God demonstrates a lack of understanding of God's creation. It seems to confuse God's gift of free will to man[18] and His command to take dominion and subdue the earth.[19] It sets aside Christ's proclamation that we would do greater works than He did.[20]

God wants us to take authority over the earth. He gave us authority here and the choice to serve Him or Satan. God wants everyone to be saved, but is everybody getting saved? No. Why? Because people have the choice to be saved or not. To receive the gift or reject it.

As an example, I will use our company as an illustration. Imagine I authorized and instructed someone in my employment, "I would like you to go and do A, B, and C." The next day that employee called me and said, "Hey Paul, I am waiting on you to move. Paul, I ask you to do A, B, and C. I will give you the glory for it. Thank you, Paul, for doing the work!"

He would not remain on the team. I would fire him.

TO ILLUSTRATE

If God has given you an assignment to do, then you best get on with it. If you stand around saying, "Have Your way, God. Move. Do it …" I picture God saying, "I can't do it because I require a body on the earth that will cooperate, which is why I need you, or someone else, to do it. Otherwise, it can't be done. Dominion of the earth has been *given* to man, and I won't take it back. I told *you* to do it. I gave *you* the authority to do it. The creativity to do it. Every resource in heaven and earth to do it."

Why would we say or sing words that deny the reality of His power, presence, and authority manifested on the earth through His sons and daughters?[21] We are His anointed ones commissioned all over the world, and rather than us waiting on Him to move, it is us who need to manifest His presence here and now so His kingdom will come on earth as it is in heaven. We are His witnesses. He has already poured out His Spirit upon us, and now we need to act upon what He is saying.

> **Why would we say or sing words that deny the reality of God's power, presence, and authority manifested on the earth through His sons and daughters?**

SOLID FOUNDATIONS

I have just scratched the surface by describing only a few commonly held fallacies that permeate the worship culture of the modern church. I could go on, but I am not trying to create a checklist of what one can and cannot say. Instead, I encourage you to be sure-footed in your theology. Have a solid foundation for your faith, then operate in love, power, and a sound mind.

You must think rightly in order to speak or sing rightly. A.W. Tozer says that what comes into our minds when we think about God is the most important thing about us. Let me share this brief excerpt by him from *The Knowledge of the Holy*:

> *The history of mankind will probably show that no people has ever risen above its religion, and man's spiritual history will positively demonstrate that no religion has ever been greater than its idea of God.* **Worship is pure or base as the worshiper entertains high or low thoughts of God.**
>
> *For this reason, the gravest question before the Church is always God Himself, and the most portentous fact about any man is not what he at a given time may say or do, but what he in his deep heart conceives God to be like.*
>
> *We tend by a secret law of the soul to move toward our mental image of God. This is true not only of the individual Christian, but of the company of Christians that compose the Church.* **Always the most revealing thing about the Church is her idea of God.**[22]

So, when you worship, what do your words communicate about what you believe about God? When you sing, what is released from your lips about your union with Christ? About your authority in Christ and your position in Christ? Where you are seated with Christ? Your priesthood as a believer? The indwelling of the Holy Spirit? All these things are fundamental to your faith. They are your foundation.

And the foundation of your faith is essential to the words you say and sing.

We must not be careless with what we release as worship. It is important that we discern the truth from lies. We must be able to identify the truth in the middle of things that sound religious and not blithely give our agreement to things that may sound harmless but dilute the power of our relationship with God.

We must not be careless with what we release as worship.

Our final chapter will briefly examine what that might look like worked out practically and invite you to try something new.

The THEFT of WORSHIP

ENDNOTES

1. Matthew 28:20, AMP.
2. See Deuteronomy 31:8, Joshua 1:5, Hebrews 13:5.
3. See Psalm 139:7-12.
4. See Numbers 14:21, Psalm 72:19, Jeremiah 23:24, Ephesians 4:10.
5. See 1 Chronicles 28:20.
6. See Psalm 46:1.
7. See Exodus 29:46, Leviticus 26:11, 1 Kings 6:13, John 1:14, Revelation 21:3
8. See Hebrews 4:16.
9. See Acts 17:28.
10. *100 Bible Verses About God Will Never Leave You or Forsake You.* https://www.openbible.info/topics/god_will_never_leave_you_or_forsake_you.
11. See Galatians 2:20.
12. See Matthew 18:20.
13. 1 John 4:17, KJV.
14. See John 5:19.
15. See Ephesians 2:10.
16. See 1 Samuel 15:22
17. See Genesis 1:26-31.
18. See Genesis 2:16-17, Joshua 24:15, Proverbs 16:9, Mark 8:34, John 7:17, Revelation 3:20.
19. See Genesis 1:28.
20. See John 14:12.
21. See Romans 8:12-25.
22. *The Knowledge of the Holy* by A.W. Tozer. Harper Collins, emphasis added.

CHAPTER 8

COME UP HIGHER

What is the Holy Spirit saying to you? God's mandate to me was crystal clear—I am not to sing or say anything Jesus would not sing or say. It's a personal conviction for me. As you finish reading my testimony and referencing scripture, we invite you to ask if this perspective might be sound biblical doctrine— especially now that we are living in the New Covenant and in the age of the Spirit. Hear God's heart on the matter. Don't just repeat the behavior you have done historically. Instead, open your mind and spirit to ask why there might be a disparity between what the Bible promises and your current reality.

Becoming dogmatic or legalistic is the exact opposite of what this book encourages. It is an invitation to freedom and a deeper level of communion with Christ. It is an invitation to activate your authority as a believer. It is an invitation to a richer, deeper relationship with the Godhead that profoundly impacts your daily life and practice. It invites you to reflect on what has been presented, line it up with scripture, and see if it resonates in your spirit. If you see truth in it, I encourage you to investigate further. Talk with the Holy Spirit. Don't default to the conformity of Western Christian orthodoxy. Be a pioneer. Be led of the Spirit and explore this territory with the heart of an adventurer.

I desire to challenge you—to see you embrace a higher experience and live in the full provision, promise, and position of being in unbroken union with Christ. I desire you to experience the best that God has for you. I want what I am experiencing every day—and even greater—to be your portion.

Before tying this all together and issuing a specific charge, let's review briefly what we have discussed.

PROGRESSIVE REVELATION

Progressive revelation holds the belief that the things God has revealed to humanity are not given all at once but in stages. The Old Testament holds truth; the New Testament does not negate this, but it builds on that foundation and expands our understanding and practice of truth. We could never enter into the New Covenant without the foundation of the Old Covenant. The latter expands the former.

God is a revealer by nature, and He reveals Himself to us through a constant unfolding of His plan and purpose. What He is saying today never negates what He has said in the past, but what He is saying today is a fuller expression. The more we know Him, the more of Him He allows us to know. It is a building, increasing revelation. We get to know things today that the saints born one hundred years ago did not know or experience.

The "mainstream" usually rejects what is "new" because it confronts what the majority has practiced until it has crystalized into normality and has become the accepted tradition. Everything mainstream was once new, perhaps radical. This publication may seem to go against the day's popular, mainstream, evangelical, conventional practices, but it is not new. It is an awakening to something that is ancient. Search your heart. Search the Word of God, and ask the Holy Spirit to confirm and clarify. Ask the Revealer to reveal Himself to you.

> **Search your heart. Search the Word of God—ask the Revealer to reveal Himself to you.**

WORDS CREATE WORLDS

Your words are a container of intention and meaning. Your words carry your thoughts, and because your thoughts originate from your heart, your words are the expression of your heart—your beliefs. Your words are "spirit containers" that hold and harness great and endless creative power. Our speech is directly related to our outcomes. We get what we say.

> **If what we say is important, then what we sing must be equally important.**

God speaks only life-giving, life-sustaining, life-generating words, and His Kingdom is established by His words. I have no desire to undo with my mouth what God has done for me by Christ's blood. By our words, we are justified, and by our words, we will be condemned, so what we say really matters. And if what we say is important, then what we sing must be equally important.

WORSHIP IS OBEDIENCE

At its core, worship is obedience. We looked at the first time worship was mentioned in the Bible and found that it was when Abram went to the top of the mountain to offer Isaac to the Lord in obedience. We discussed that there is acceptable worship, and if there is acceptable worship, there must also be worship that is not acceptable.

We place our lives before God as an offering, presenting our bodies as a holy and living sacrifice, giving Him our all. Poured out. Emptied. Bowed down in honor and reverence. All that we have and all that we are belongs to Him, with nothing held back. We give Him total lordship of our mind, our will, and our intellect, and everything within our stewardship is to be managed according to His voice and for His glory. Just as a literal sacrifice was slaughtered and placed on an altar to be burned, we are to place our soul on a spiritual altar to be consumed by the fire of His holy presence.

Worship must be done in spirit and in truth. And to be done in truth, both our hearts and heads must be engaged in what we are singing and saying and doing. These must align with who God is and who we are in Him.

EXPRESSING LOVE IN OUR OWN WORDS

We discussed prayer and demonstrated the difference between reading a prayer from a book and speaking authentically and originally to God from our hearts. I gave an example of how my spouse would feel if I sent her a letter written by someone else and just signed my name at the bottom. Would that be acceptable? No, we must use our own words to express our love.

So, if we don't usually use other people's words when we pray, why would we do this when we worship? You don't have to be a poet or a linguist to worship with your own words from your own heart. "For out of the heart, the mouth speaks."[1] If you are struggling to express yourself, when you are out of words, or when the words you have are insufficient, then sing in tongues. When you sing in the Spirit, there is no limit to your vocabulary, phrasing, or facts of your expression.

SOLID FOUNDATIONS

If someone is a brand-new believer in Christ and does not yet know who they are in Christ and is still grappling with their carnal nature, having a primer to guide them makes sense.

Singing songs composed for them is helpful. But please, let the lyrics be accurate and theologically correct.

Singing doctrinally sound songs that agree with our position in Christ is never a problem. It's a good reminder and a great devotional practice. But troubles arise when we mindlessly sing along to lyrics projected on a screen that are in conflict with the foundations of our faith. So, knowing who you are and what you believe is important. Your foundation in Christ must be solid and secure, and you must be able to quickly discern if what you are releasing from your mouth is in alignment with the New Covenant reality of your relationship with God or not.

Basic theology is the responsibility of every believer. I encourage every person who writes and releases songs meant to be sung as praise and worship to measure them against sound biblical doctrine. If they do not align, it would be far better for those songs to remain personal and composed and privately sung before God in season, as you would do while processing private pain or struggle in a journal, rather than releasing them to the masses.

We are responsible for the words we release.

THE CHARGE

In chapter five, I shared my experience with the baptism in the Holy Ghost and invited you to receive that gift, or if you already have it, to exercise it with greater diligence. Baptism in the Spirit is the on-ramp to the supernatural. There is access to incredible power to live abundantly, to walk worthy, to please God, and to commune with Him in ways that surpass understanding.

So, the practical solution for handling corporate gatherings where the songs being sung do not agree with what Jesus would sing or say is really quite simple. When these songs are being sung, we are much better off singing our own lyrics or praying or singing in the Spirit than releasing words from our mouths that undermine God's presence alive and at work in us.

That's it. The entire setup of the book comes down to this simple adjustment.

We don't have to push this practice on other people or make a doctrine out of it. We certainly don't want to walk around in judgment or condemn others. We—Father, Son, Holy Spirit, *and* Paul Allen—humbly and respectfully invite you to consider whether the words you sing or say release you into God's fullness or limit your experience. We invite you to consider if some of what the mainstream has billed as *worship* music might not be worship at all. And if you reach that conclusion, then we challenge you to adjust your practice for the next thirty days.

Do the words you sing and say release you into abundant life or limit your experience?

Over the next month, pay careful attention to your words. Accept this charge to speak or sing *only* words that Jesus could speak or sing—words that align with you speaking *as* Christ, not *for* Him. When music is sung around you that you cannot sing, sing your own words. Sometimes all that is required is a minor edit to make the lyrics compatible with your position in Christ. For example, instead of singing, "Welcome, Holy Spirit, into this place," you can adjust it to say, "I'm delighted, Holy Spirit, you are in this place," and point to your belly as you do.

Best of all, sing in the Spirit, and you cannot go wrong. Tongues is God-language. Undefiled. Inerrant.

The expression of God's Spirit language—tongues—is far superior to the English language, or any other language for that matter. Words cannot adequately express how good He is. No human language on earth can give sufficient expression to our worship.

> **No human language on earth can give sufficient expression to our worship.**

Heavenly language is without limitation, and it is all-sufficient. Go ahead, sing in the Spirit. Does it feel awkward at first? That's okay. Does it not make sense to your carnal, natural mind? That's okay, too. It is your spirit, not your mind, that is communing with the Father. It is perfectly acceptable for your mind to lack understanding in this while your spirit is fruitful.[2]

As you pray and sing in the Spirit, your spirit will be built up and edified,[3] and your heavenly Father will be delighted. You can't get it wrong because your spirit is conversing directly with God's Spirit.

COME UP HIGHER

I have now done this personally for years, and the practice has brought me to a place in my spirit where I am so aware of my God-nature that my old human nature and its desires have become a thing of the past. They are not even a distant memory. I am enjoying my new life in Christ Jesus with all its rights and privileges, and the way to access it all is by praying and singing in the Spirit.

As you embrace this opportunity, I caution you to resist the human tendency to become "better-than-thou" when you have experienced something others have not yet encountered. Refrain from becoming antagonistic or critical. The Christians beside you are all in different places, and our job is to encourage them.

When you find yourself in corporate worship, and you recognize that the lyrics are limiting, smile, have joy, and sing to your Father from the depths of your heart with words that you know will please Him. It's not illegal to borrow someone else's words, and there is power in the unity of corporate expression at appropriate times. But it's pretty lame if you can't thank God without having someone prescribe the words to you. Do you love God? Are you grateful to Him for who He is and what He has done? Then tell Him directly.

It's pretty lame if you can't thank God without having someone prescribe the words to you.

Sing to Him directly.

The THEFT *of* WORSHIP

He loves it when you do so.

Try it for thirty days and see what happens. In thirty days, I believe you will see a breakthrough.

You will see heaven come to earth. You will experience a new dimension of supernatural revelation and understanding. Doors will open. Answers will come. Mountains will move, and you will be changed.

ENDNOTES

1. Matthew 12:34, NKJV.
2. See 1 Corinthians 14:14.
3. Ibid.

ABOUT THE AUTHOR

Paul Allen graduated Summa Cum Laude from Zion Bible College, President of the Class of 2004, and Magna Cum Laude with a Masters in Ministry from Gordon-Conwell Theological Seminary in 2010. He has served in various ministerial capacities in Massachusetts since 2000 and in Texas since 2015.

Paul and his wife, Yvonne, exemplify practical Christian living, putting God first in every decision. They have a wonderful marriage, a great family, and a successful business. They have two married children with growing, thriving families of their own. Paul and Yvonne are blessed to be a blessing and love sharing the abundant life with others.

To contact the author:

PAUL@THE29THCHAPTER.COM

There's insufficient verbiage
To well describe our state
Oneness with the Trinity
This new God-man innate

God, You are so good to us
Words so hard to find
Glad for *glossolalia*—
Words beyond our mind

Thank You for this parlance
Straight from heart to heart
Happily expressing
Lord, how great Thou art

Eternity now is in our hearts
Forever now, we live
Greatest thanks to You we bring
Our lives, to You we give

Abba, You're so good to us
All breathing gives You thanks
Oneness with us, we declare
Resounding 'cross the ranks

So good, so good
Abba, You're so good

—PAUL ALLEN

Made in the USA
Columbia, SC
13 August 2024